NO, YOU
TELL IT!

Subscribe to the No, YOU Tell It! podcast to listen to the live performances of the story swaps featured in the ten-year anthology and more. Available at noyoutellit.com and all major platforms.

Join the mailing list at palmcirclepress.net to receive advanced notice of new releases and for the chance to receive FREE books.

PALM CIRCLE PRESS

NO, YOU TELL IT!

TEN-YEAR ANTHOLOGY
2022

EDITED BY
KELLY JEAN FITZSIMMONS

Printed in the United States of America

ISBN: 978-1-7359325-8-3

Book Design by Oladimerji Alaka
Interior Design by Rachel Newhouse for elfinpen design

Published by Palm Circle Press
palmcirclepress.net

No, YOU Tell It! front cover logo by Joshua Dunn and Noah Diamond; *No, YOU Tell It!* interior ten-year anniversary logo by Noah Diamond.

"SeeyouinthemorningIloveyougoodnight." by Molly Touger, developed as part of *No, YOU Tell It!* "In Transit" in July 2013, was first published in *The Literary Review via TLR SHARE*.

"A Midwestern Purgatory" by Heather Lang-Cassera was developed as part of *No, YOU Tell It!* "No Regrets" in August 2016 and a version of this essay first appeared in *From Pantyhose to Spandex: Writers on the Job Redux* (Serving House Books, 2017) Edited by Thomas E. Kennedy and Walter Cummins.

"Viva La Curl-Volution" by Michele Carlo, developed as part of *No, YOU Tell It!* "What I Know" in March 2022, was first published as "Exactly Like Nobody" for the Puerto Rican Writers Folio: *A Hauntology*, published in Big Other in June 2022.

This anthology is dedicated to Erika Iverson, Mike Dressel, and Tim Lindner. *No, YOU Tell It!* wouldn't exist today without you, and I am forever grateful.

Special thanks to Lisa Fitzsimmons Eddins, Jeff Wills, and Lee Anderson for the emotional and editorial support bringing these beautiful pages together.

All my love to our alumni storytellers, audience members, and everyone who has supported our series over the past decade.

CONTENTS

FOREWORD

Kelly Jean Fitzsimmons

No, YOU Tell It! (NYTI) *is a nonfiction development and reading series where storytellers first work together to create their true tales on the page, then swap stories to embody each other's experiences on stage. We value cooperation over competition, supporting participants as they produce personal stories from the inside out.*

*

I have been working on our *NYTI* elevator pitch for the past ten years—for approaching potential storytellers, for marketing materials, for our website (once we got one). Hell, I've even recited it in an elevator. But no elevator ride seems long enough. It is impossible to capture all the connection, knowledge, laughter, tears, and joy *No, YOU Tell It!* manifests before the doors open and the ride ends.

The series began as an experiment in 2012 when I gathered four friends with varied creative backgrounds—Jorge Cordova, David Harrell, Jeremy Holmes, and Erika Iverson—to provide artistic and emotional scaffolding for each other as they wrote and traded true tales. All four brought in stories that wrestled with their different religious upbringings. Thus the first show theme, "Religion," was born.

That show is also an origin story for one of my favorite aspects of *No, YOU Tell It!* We'd rented a small studio space for the performance and were running out of room for the audience, so I asked the storytellers to sit up on stage. Afterward, so many people shared how much they loved watching the author's face as their partner performed their story, we've had the story partners sit up on stage together ever since.

No, YOU Tell It! is unique in that it asks participants to tell each other's stories. There is an extra effort involved, but there is also a kind of freedom. For that first show, Erika wrote a raw story about her mother's recent death. At one point in developing it she turned to her story partner, Jorge, and said, "I don't think I can read this out loud. But I can let you read it."

When I rehearsed the story with Jorge, making theatrical choices as to how Erika's mother's voice would sound and how to best honor the deep mixture of anger and grief on the page, I kept thinking of how glad I was to be rehearsing with him, and not Erika herself. After the show, Erika expressed relief over facing her anger "by proxy," and gratitude to Jorge for being willing to go through the experience for her.

I knew that night we had something special in *No, YOU Tell It!*, and asked Erika to stay on the creative team as a director. We chose the ironic theme of "Firsts" for our second show, which brought us our third original team member in Mike Dressel, as story coach and literary voice of reason. Over the past decade, we have worked with close to 200 artists (authors, actors, poets, comedians, visual artists, photographers, musicians, magicians, and more), as well as encouraged people who might not have experience writing, performing, or both, to tell their stories.

This anthology is not just a showcase of personal stories. It also highlights the evolution of the series to tell the story of *No, YOU Tell It!* itself. These pages demonstrate how a unique level of empathy is generated as the storytellers embody their story partner's culture, identity, perspective, and life experience. The desire to honor your partner's story as much as your own strengthens the written narrative and empowers the literary citizenship of storytellers and audience members alike. The *No, YOU Tell It! Ten-Year Anthology 2022* is my elevator up into the sky, and there still isn't enough time to share all the ways this past decade has enriched our lives, but I hope you enjoy the ride.

URBAN DWELLERS

November 12th, 2012
Jimmy's No. 43 | New York City

Podcast Episode 1

"Monograph Series"
written by Alexandra Gray
and performed by Fred Backus

"GG Allin Says Goodbye"
written by Fred Backus
and performed by Alexandra Gray

Kelly Jean Fitzsimmons | Series Creator and Producer

Location, Location, Location!

When charged with elevating *No, YOU Tell It!* from an experiment to a regular series, that old real estate saying became *Venue, Venue, Venue!* The audience reaction to our first show was so positive that everyone involved encouraged me to continue. Great. Except, where would we do our little show that could?

I couldn't commit to a "first Tuesday of every month" type of series, which was what most of the venues I contacted wanted. *No, YOU Tell It!* isn't the kind of event where participants simply show up on the night of to share their words. First, we curate a group of four storytellers and ask them to write an original true tale inspired by a simple but evocative theme. The *NYTI* creative team leads them through two story workshops where they read each other's drafts out loud and receive group feedback to inform their revisions. Next, each storyteller rehearses with their assigned director to practice embodying their story partner's tale as their own for the live show. This all takes months of lead-time.

We needed a space open to sporadic shows. One that complemented the theatrical nature of our series but could be quiet enough to honor the empathetic connections created by switching stories. Most importantly, it had to be FREE.

Back then, we were funded solely by volunteered efforts and swiped office supplies from my day job. A friend connected me with the event booker at Jimmy's No. 43, an East Village beer and cider bar with a cellar-like back room doubling as a performance space. The booker agreed to a quarterly schedule, one show about every three months, and Jimmy's became our first, free home. Of course, to quote another hackneyed phrase, "There's no such thing as a free lunch." Or venue it seems!

Producing our show at Jimmy's No. 43 came with two major caveats. The first was that each September, I had to provide the event booker with all of our show dates for the entire upcoming calendar year and stick to them. In hindsight, I recognize this pain point as one of the most instrumental aids in helping me get the series off the ground. The forced regularity provided a stable spine, holding me up as a producer, which allowed me to concentrate on curating the series and fine-tuning our collaborative workshop process.

The second caveat, a far more farcical price to pay when producing a show in a bar, was the barback always, ALWAYS came in to change a keg during the most intimate, gut-wrenching part of the story being performed. Hosting the show, all I could do was throw flames from my eyes toward my team and mentally will the loud CLANKS and shrill SQUEAKS to, "Just stop already!"

What better setting could there have been for the "Urban Dwellers" theme of one of our earliest shows? Even when they changed the damn keg during Alexandra Gray's "Monograph Series," you could feel the audience coming together. Heads tilted so as not to miss a single word from story partner Fred Backus of her poignant memory play on the work of artist Mark Rothko.

In turn, the drunken squawks of laughter floating in from the bar and mysterious muddy drips of water falling on our heads created the perfect ambiance for Fred's visceral tale of attending punk rocker GG Allin's last show before his death. Filled with the notorious stage antics the musician was known for, Fred's story of leaving his punk-rock youth behind is also a love letter to the beautiful ugliness of the Lower East Side that once was.

Reliving these journeys in the back of a leaky, subterranean bar that soon joined the ranks of vanishing New York was imperfectly perfect. When Jimmy's closed in 2017, I knew I'd miss those noisy nights. Miss being crowded into the back room, swapping stories in that tight square of a stage, with only one working spotlight, and a chalkboard back wall forever smeared with dusty pink-and-white echoes of lost letters that refused to be wiped clean. I am grateful

Jimmy's No. 43 gave us a home those first few years and hope you enjoy a bit of the magic from that night.

MONOGRAPH SERIES

ALEXANDRA GRAY

mon·o·graph   [mon-uh-graf, -grahf]: noun, a treatise on a particular subject, as a biographical study or study of the works of one artist.

Museum of Modern Art, New York City: *No. 16 (Red, Brown, and Black)*, Mark Rothko

I turn a corner and the painting is suddenly in front of me: giant, heavy, unmovable. Three dark rectangles stare down, momentarily overwhelming my senses. I look down at the floor, then up. I breathe in. I am here. My feet are on the floor. I breathe out.

In old movies, when someone loses their job, they always go to Central Park, probably because they don't know where else to go. They've lost their routine, their rhythm. This is my routine. If I am in any city with a painting by Mark Rothko I go and visit it, like an old friend. It's not so much about the artist himself—Rothko is long dead and I don't feel a huge kinship with him as a person—but his paintings vibrate off the canvas, jump forward at me, tell stories, state facts with their mute and determined lack of figure. If anything, it's these inanimate objects I feel a kinship with, though to me the term "inanimate" doesn't apply at all. Each work has a life, a beating heart. I am drawn like a magnet and would stand in front of his paintings all day if I could.

And now I *have* all day! Oh. Good. No reason to be anywhere at 9 a.m. or 10 a.m. or even noon. Days, then weeks line up in front of me, all empty, like legions of inflatable question marks cascading into the infinite sky.

I focus on practical things, like feeding myself. An inventory of my apartment reveals that I have lots of old rice in jars. If I lived in *Little House on the Prairie* it would be infested with weevils by now, but thanks to the miracle of modern food storage it's still edible. I make a note to make lots of rice dishes.

But I am not much of a cook. In the few days since my dismissal I have subsisted on the kinds of dishes that appear in children's cookbooks—foods that require assembly only, as opposed to the dangerous use of flame or heat. I'm eating starter foods, as I myself am starting over. The only difference between me now and me at six years old is that the banana slices on my toast are no longer arranged in a smiley face. If they were arranged to express my state of mind, the eye slices would be bruised to illustrate lack of sleep; the mouth would be cut slim as lips pressed hard together by anxiety. There would be eyebrows, probably made out of rice, raised upward to indicate indecision, or fear.

There is a "stress scale" developed by Thomas Holmes and Richard Rahe, two prominent psychiatrists, to measure the impact of various life events on a person's psychological well-being. According to the scale, the sudden loss of a job is comparable to a grievous bodily injury. I stand in the gallery and wonder if this is what phantom limb syndrome feels like.

Tate Modern, London: *Seagram's Mural Series*

At some point I will stop being surprised at the emotional weight of these visits. But not yet. It's 1999 and visiting London is still like visiting the past—my own and my mother's. This is her home, the city where she was born, spent most of the war, and grew into the woman who married my father and moved to the States. London is simultaneously familiar—I feel more at home here than in some of the places I've actually lived—and strange, like it doesn't belong to me.

At the Tate, I beeline to the Rothko gallery. When I sit down on the bench in the center of the room, I begin to cry. The paintings are vast, unfathomable, and I am dwarfed in comparison. They are from Rothko's later career. His pictures got darker and darker and then he cut his wrists. I breathe in, then out.

This Christmas is the first I have ever spent in London. I feel so grateful for the welcoming embrace of my cousins, who share a great deal of history with me despite growing up on different continents. There is also the shared vernacular of English Christmas: pudding, sherry, crackers, paper hats, and day drinking. But there is also a deeper vocabulary that I don't share, locked just beneath the surface that only my uncle, aunt, and cousins speak. *They* are a family. They spend every Christmas together. I'm just a relation.

I'm probably being melodramatic; they are so loving and generous. They know why I'm here. Maybe I *want* to feel like an outsider. Maybe I don't want to be part of the family without my mother. Standing in front of the paintings I feel none of that. I am completely at home and completely absorbed.

On Christmas Day, I pad downstairs in the official uniform of English Christmas: birds-nest hair and pajamas. My cousin Clare follows, outdoing me with a set of plush reindeer antlers on a headband. Alfie, only a year and a half old, is already playing with a toy Hoover. Gleefully, he shoves the hose attachment in his mouth and hums until he laughs. Torn wrapping paper soon makes a shambles of the carefully decorated living room, and every gift is exclaimed over, including the ones I brought. We break out the chocolates and sherry and I am put to work in the kitchen on the long slog towards Christmas dinner. Once it's over and we're lying about like sedated walruses, my uncle suggests a game. We consume a bit more sherry while guessing the names of celebrities based on a series of verbal clues. I feel useless, unable to recognize the names of footballers and stars of UK reality television. I manage to stump everyone with a few American celebrities, but that's not the point of the game—it's about drawing connections and finding common ground. Clearly, I'm still somewhere else.

Houston, Texas: *Rothko Chapel*

The cab driver drops me off and I feel a momentary thrill: *I made it.* It's so cold and quiet here, away from the center of the city. It's 2008. I'm in Houston for a conference, which is … fine. Today I escaped from the pacifying blandness of the hotel, skipping the morning session to come here. I look around. The neighborhood is residential, a riot of crisp orange leaves. I turn, walk to the chapel, and open the door. It is even colder and quieter inside, and it is everything I hoped it would be. The walls are grey concrete and I am surrounded by Rothko's paintings. These contain no distinct boxes of color. They're smooth, monochromatic, colossal. A glass panel overhead provides the only light.

I sit on a bench; it's heavy dark wood that feels well-worn under my palms. My eyes glide over every surface in the chapel, consuming the quiet, the cool air. I breathe in, then out. I can't believe I'm in Texas. The Rothko Chapel is understated, quiet, humble — everything Texas is not. I had to take a cab here because *surprise!* Houston is not a walking city. I walk anyway and come across some gorgeous old neon signs and theater marquees, all of them on buildings that are boarded up. I take a few pictures, knowing they won't be here for long. The photos create a parallel narrative to the frantic whirlwind of the conference. Instead of four exhausting days spent taking notes and introducing myself, I will remember bold red neon letters splashed above curved glass, a pop art sculpture rising from thick green grass, my own face reflected in the cracked mirror of a mosaic. They remind me that the job where I spend 45 hours a week, the one that threatens to crush my creative life under its wheels, isn't what defines me. The camera, a stand-in for the lenses and shutters of my own eyes, creates the space where I exist, and the possibility of escape.

I lose track of how long I've been sitting in the chapel. Only one other visitor comes in while I'm there, and she leaves before I do. I get up slowly and take a last look around. No pictures allowed. There's a little pool outside the chapel, and I stare into its glassy water for a while until I start to feel self-conscious. I pull the cab driver's card out of my pocket and call the number.

Museum of Modern Art, New York City: *No. 3/ No. 13 (Magenta, Black, Green on Orange)*

This painting hangs right next to *No. 16*—the dark one I was gazing at just a few days ago. Still no job. But *No. 3/ No. 13* is an undeniably joyful work: a bright and gushy juxtaposition to the dark vortex next door. It was created in the prime of Rothko's career, shortly after he perfected the colorblock format that became his signature. Rothko was born in what used to be Latvia, now part of Russia. But upon arriving in the States, he assimilated completely and became strongly identified with New York.

I am a city girl like my mother, even though I began life in the Berkeley Hills of California and spent my childhood in various suburbs, which were for the most part indistinguishable from one another. When people ask, "Where are you from?" I feel compelled to give a hurried compound answer: "CaliforniatheNorthwest-PennsylvaniathenNewYork."

I have lived in New York City for nearly twenty years. My roots go deeper, stretch further, but I only have a tentative grip on the first few places in my origin story. The roots that anchor me in New York are newer but much stronger, grown hard with callouses and a bit of scar tissue. If I want to, I can give the short answer: "I'm a New Yorker. This is home."

I take the city for granted, as with anything familiar. I become enraged at the same clichéd laundry list of gripes making every New Yorker occasionally contemplate escape: the expense, noise, traffic, crowds, crime, corruption, and GOOD GOD WHAT IS THAT SMELL? *IS THAT SHIT? HUMAN SHIT??* But since losing my job, New York has taken care of me in a way I didn't know I needed until I did. I wandered into Central Park a few days ago and ended up in front of the Bethesda Fountain, staring at the lilies in the pool. It was familiar. I'd seen it at night with its angel wings silhouetted against the sky.

In the past I made wishes there on my birthday. I visit the fountain, like Rothko's paintings, because I belong to them, just as I like to think they belong to me.

13

On September 11th I was in London visiting my family—in fact, I was sitting next to my cousin Clare as we watched the Towers turn to rubble on TV. The buildings, the city, were falling apart and all I wanted to do was be there. When I finally arrived a few days later, after a surreal flight where I'm pretty sure everyone was drunk, I was approached by a stranger. She must have seen my eyes as I stumbled to the cab stand with my bags. She reached for my hand and said very deliberately, "Welcome home."

I'm on the fourth floor of the MoMA, my eyes tracing the explosions of orange and magenta in *No. 3/No. 13*. People are swarming around me but I don't move. I am trying to absorb the joy, the optimism in these colors. I take in the space, the quiet, until it's not outside of me anymore. I feel the gallery floor under my feet. I breathe in, then out.

GG ALLIN SAYS GOODBYE

FRED BACKUS

We stood outside, not sure if we were going to attend. I was more reluctant than Mark. It was seven bucks—that was kind of a lot of money for a show back then. GG strode past us wearing nothing but combat boots, a leather jock strap, a jean jacket, and a Nazi helmet. Our decision was made. We were going in. GG Allin and the Murder Junkies were in town.

GG Allin—Manchester, New Hampshire's greatest contribution to Rock-n-Roll. In the late 70s, he was doing catchy pop-punk ditties until something seemed to snap inside him in the 80s. His vocal range dropped an octave, turning what was once a snotty whine into a guttural growl. His subject matter had changed as well. What first came off as teenaged rebellion had now transformed into a seething embodiment of violence, degradation, and depravity. Take, for example, the lyrics to a song called "Teenaged Twats:"

Hey little girl, you squeak when you walk
I want to tie you up and shit on your face

Or "Die When You Die:"

Die when you die when you die when you die,
If you get AIDS spread it around and take some lives

You get the idea.

However, the GG Allin songbook paled in comparison to the GG Allin stage act. He was known for performing naked. Rumor had it that he took laxatives before shows to ensure he had an ample supply of fecal matter to fling at the audience. The stories were legendary. That he once shat on a biscuit and ate it. That he once sucked his own brother's dick onstage. Between moments of self-degradation, he would assault people. He once grabbed a woman by the hair and dragged her between his legs and took a crap on her head. He beat people up and often got beat up in return. He didn't care. Sid Vicious may have been punk's most notorious nihilist, but GG Allin was its purest.

He announced he would commit suicide on stage on October 31st, 1990, and it was generally assumed he would take everyone in attendance out with him. He didn't make the date because he was in prison for tying up his girlfriend and lighting her on fire. It was only because he was out of jail now that he was playing New York.

It was 1993, and we were standing outside a spot called the Gas Station on the corner of Avenue B and 2nd Street. It was, in fact, an abandoned gas station, but it wasn't the sort of refurbished theme venue you might expect to find these days. Instead, it had been pretty much left to decay "as is" until some local artists transformed it, surrounding it and filling it with sculptures made from welded metal and other discarded debris—one of many such sculpture gardens dotting the vacant lots and reclaimed gardens of the Lower East Side. Space and material were plentiful back then, especially if you were willing to recycle what others had thrown away. Sculptors in the neighborhood made good use of both and created some astonishing works of art.

The junk tower on 6th Street rose a couple of stories high—a towering beacon of trash turned to art—calling attention to what the city had given up on, and later telling the bulldozers where to show up when it was time to take it all back. The Gas Station was both a physical product and a symbol of the neighborhood for that time.

Hard to imagine a time when real estate in this city wasn't in a constant state of redevelopment, but back in the late 80s, which was around the time I discovered there was a neighborhood in Manhattan where the avenues ran out of numbers, the city seemed positively primeval compared to the way it is now. I had been coming downtown since I was about fourteen or so, drawn there from the relative safety of Westchester. The Central and East Villages became the pilgrimage destination for kids into certain types of music throughout the Tri-State Region and beyond.

My poison was punk rock, and in Dobbs Ferry, there were two of us, just Mark and me, and as we got older, we found ourselves being drawn east to the abandoned lots and buildings where the scene was a little wilder and more authentic. Eventually, we ended up in a band together called The Casualties, and I soon found myself inside the wild and chaotic punk scene of the Lower East Side.

We had played the Gas Station a year before the GG Allin show. A lot of our shows were at places like that, abandoned warehouses and squats. My first official gig with The Casualties was at a squat called Lucky 13, and we found out about the show because the squatters who lived there had put up flyers around the neighborhood with our band in the line-up, hoping we'd show up. The neighborhood was filled with squats back then, which mostly orbited Tompkins Square Park like planets around a dying star.

The block where Lucky 13 was situated, 13th Street between A and B, must have had at least a half-dozen squats on that stretch alone. I always felt the squats were in some ways the heart and soul of the neighborhood—a neighborhood that was dangerous, dirty, and infested with junkies. Yet it was also infested with life—punks, artists, writers, drag queens—a swirling sea of creative and anarchic forces that was still the Lower East Side.

It couldn't last. By the time GG Allin played the Gas Station in 1993, the writing was on the wall. A series of violent confrontations with the forces of gentrification had been taking place for a few years around Tompkins Square Park since the 1988 riot. The last big uprising of resistance would be in 1995, when the 13th Street squats were cleared out by the NYPD in riot gear. It was the neighborhood's last stand. The Squatter Little Big Horn.

The squats are all gone now, as are pretty much all of the denizens and watering holes of the old Lower East Side. It's strange to find yourself missing a city you never left, walking around it in circles year-by-year and watching it slip away a little more with every step to the concrete. I found myself on the Lower East Side on a Sunday not long ago, trying to remember where everything was. There are no vacant lots or abandoned buildings. Spots like Downtown Beirut or the Lismar Lounge have been replaced by restaurants where you can spend twenty bucks on a two-egg omelet or bars filled with meatheads in football jerseys watching big-screen TVs. There is a Duane Reade on the corner of 2nd Street and Avenue B where the Gas Station once stood, and it too now stands as a neighborhood symbol.

I don't know what happened to all the scrap art sculptures that used to adorn the Gas Station. I wasn't spending much time thinking about them back in 1993 as I went in to see GG Allin. I didn't think about them much until they were gone. Instead, I was thinking about getting a broken nose or getting covered in shit. I was ambivalent about being there. I suppose it was an event that was not to be missed, but a hard one to justify. It felt somehow morally irresponsible like eagerly watching a car wreck, and that was only if you were lucky enough not to end up as roadkill yourself. Truth be told, I wasn't even really a part of that scene anymore. I was out of the band and in college in Connecticut by this time, just back for the summer—one foot in and one foot out. My aspirations were elsewhere, as were many of my friends. Our pals The Denied were the opening act, which was another reason I was there. I guess I saw them play, I don't remember. GG Allin and the Murder Junkies wiped away any memory of their set.

I do remember when the Murder Junkies started to play it was loud and in no time, GG was out there in nothing but combat boots and a dog collar. Once he got naked it was hard not to notice that he had an impossibly small dick—a dick so small you couldn't even see that he had one at first. Whether this explained anything about his psyche I didn't have time to ponder because things started to get going, and I can't remember whether his fists or his shit started flying first. I think it was his fists. He savagely punched a guy in the face almost immediately, still clutching the microphone after growling out the first verse of a song. Then dirty brown liquid started exploding from his ass, a clumpy, soupy mixture he smeared all over his naked body. He wailed on a few people who got too close, punching them in the face. I guess some people in the front didn't expect him to live up to the hype.

Most staggered away dazed from the blows. Those who decided to fight back were quickly taken out by the bouncers, who sadly were friends of ours, intoxicated by the violence and their momentary positions of power. It was bullshit, frankly. If you were going to open up the floodgates of violence, you shouldn't have just been able to dish it out without it coming back to you.

It was hard to feel too bad for the wounded, however. Like the Running of the Bulls, we all fully deserved whatever was coming to us just by being there. It was not as if we hadn't been warned. That was why I didn't feel sorry for the giggling girl taking photos up in front. She didn't comprehend what exactly we were dealing with here. GG took a clump of shit in one hand, pulled her camera down with his other hand, and shoved the clump into her face. She was still giggling. I guess she didn't know what else to do.

By this point he was flinging clumps of feces into the audience indiscriminately like a crazed gorilla—at the people who, like me, had hoped against hope they could see this business through without getting down and dirty with GG. He charged the audience, and it was a pretty remarkable thing to see a hundred or so people running in actual fear from one solitary naked man. There were still a few people whom he didn't fuck with, however. Some of the squatter punks, the real deals, not guys like me who had one foot in and one foot out, the guys who were singing along to the songs right up front and center … for whom GG Allin wasn't just a freak or a novelty or an anecdote, but for whom GG Allin actually meant something.

For all the things he could be reviled for, GG Allin was perhaps as true an expression of counterculture and non-conformity as you could conceive of, living fully in the moment, without regard to the future, searching for that moment where the primal forces of creation and destruction meet.

As for me, I was headed in a different direction. Was I a poseur? Well, in context perhaps I was, but the bar was set pretty high. Maybe it was this realization, or the bleeding people around me, or the shower of fecal matter that splattered Mark's arm, that convinced me it was time to go. I was not punk rock enough for GG Allin. I decided I was okay with that. I had lasted seven minutes. A dollar a minute by my reckoning. The show didn't last much longer.

It was still daylight, and there were plenty of people who fled before me, mingling on the street. More were to follow. They came in waves. You'd hear screams from inside the garage, and then through the gaps in the scrap metal, you'd see the audience run in terror into the yard. Slowly they'd creep back in, but in ever dwindling numbers. I'm not sure how many rounds Mark lasted, but I'm pretty sure he was outside when, after one particularly loud and prolonged batch of crashing and screaming, the bouncers carried someone out, unconscious but twitching, dropping him in the gutter on 2nd Street. After that point, most of the audience had fled for good; there was just a handful of the furriest and filthiest left inside. The band was no longer playing because someone had cut the power. Finally, GG himself appeared, striding out into Avenue B in nothing but his biker books and his own feces—a motley assortment of his most faithful marching behind him while chanting: "GG! GG! GG!" directly toward the panicked passengers of a city bus heading south on Avenue B.

GG threw himself in the street in front of the bus, after which his followers unleashed a barrage of glass bottles at it. The bus helplessly tried getting away amidst the blaring sirens of the soon-to-be-arriving police force. When they threw bottles at the cops, things started to get ugly, though GG was no longer on the scene by then.

One night years ago we stood drinking 40s outside of Mona's on Avenue B when a guy we called "Limey Shawn" told me his Philosophy of Punk: "When someone tells you not to smash a bottle against a car, you smash it against your own face." It's not a philosophy for living to a ripe old age. It's the here and now, relentless and unforgiving. By its nature, it can't last. For GG Allin this would be his final blaze of glory. His Little Big Horn. He overdosed on heroin later that night. His appearance at the Gas Station marked not just his last show but his ultimate act on Earth— a bulb burning brightly before burning itself out—leaving blood, shit, and broken glass in his wake.

It signaled the beginning of the end of an era. For me, for the neighborhood, certainly for GG Allin—an unrepentant explosion of spirit—a pus-filled boil spraying out the creativity, the filth, the danger, and the beautiful ugliness that still existed but not for much longer. Soon to be paved away like everything else, along with all the blood, shit, and broken glass.

IN TRANSIT

July 30th, 2013
Jimmy's No. 43 | New York City

Podcast Episode 24

"One Car: $2500"
written by Brian Hutchinson
and performed by Colby Black

"My God, What Have I Done?"
written by Colby Black
and performed by Brian Hutchinson

Podcast Episode 11

"SeeyouinthemorningIloveyougoodnight."
written by Molly Touger
and performed by Rebecca Hart

"Song Lines"
written by Rebecca Hart
and performed by Molly Touger

Erika Iverson | Director and Founding Member

The first story meeting of each *No, YOU Tell It!* cohort is always exciting, unknown territory. There is a fizzy "first day of school" feeling. *What will these people be like? What will their stories be?* Ideally, we find people who don't already know each other, as we want to have a diversity of writing styles and perspectives in the room. We don't know what stories the show theme has inspired people to write until the four storytellers read each other's drafts aloud. A kind of alchemical magic occurs when everyone first comes together.

Each company of *NYTI* storytellers has its own flavor. Kelly Jean works hard to curate the group; one bad carrot really can spoil the soup! As many of us have experienced in other writers' workshops, if just one person comes in with a snotty attitude or an unwillingness to participate, the temperature and tempo in the room can change from a fun, supportive vibe to a frosty stillness. It's a testament to Kelly Jean's careful curation that in ten years we've never had this happen.

What we never anticipated happening, however, was having two storytellers walk into that first meeting with the same story in hand. Colby Black and Brian Hutchinson brought in distinct yet perfectly parallel "In Transit" stories of their love affairs with cars. Colby's story was read aloud first, and it wasn't until the end of the evening that we heard Brian's. At the beginning, we all giggled, assuming the look of discomfort on his face was because his was *another* story about buying a car on eBay. The big laugh in the room came at the end of the story, causing Brian to bury his face in his hands. Turns out, Brian was less concerned about having the same plot as Colby and more about the denouement—where he nicknamed his car "Erica" and proclaimed that all Ericas are "a little bitchy." Snorting with laughter, I reassured him:

a) "Ericas" were vastly different from "Erikas," and

b) it was probably true.

We knew we had to pair Brian and Colby as our first story swap of the evening. How could we not? But could we give their performances enough *oomph* so audiences didn't feel like they were sitting through the same story twice?

As a *No, YOU Tell It!* director working with storytellers whose performance experience varies, the basic instructions I provide are similar to those I gave at the Catholic high school where I taught drama: Stand solidly on two feet, try not to sway too much, and put your hands on the music stand when you don't know what to do with them. I remind them to slow down and give their listeners time to catch up. We usually don't use microphones, so I ask storytellers to imagine their slightly deaf Aunt Ethel sitting in the back row: "She really wants to hear every word. Don't disappoint Aunt Ethel! She came a long way to hear you perform!"

Any hesitation Brian might have expressed in our first meeting about needing to be polite was gone when it came time for rehearsal. Both incredibly charismatic people, he and Colby were game to go big. They embraced both the absurdity of their story similarities and embodied each other's rhythmic punch lines. Listening to the audio from that evening, you can hear the audience howling, even over the inevitable keg change and extra-rowdy bar sounds from the next room. And, yes, the line about bitchy "Erica" paid off. Aunt Ethel was rolling in the aisles.

Are these stories really about the same thing? Brian's classic travelogue keeps us in suspense—will he make it back in time for his lab the next morning? Colby's story tells us relatively little about the actual journey and more about what awaited him on the other side. But eventually, both cars bring our friends to the present day, making their current lives possible. They are vehicles to the future for both of our charming storytellers, and I couldn't be happier for them.

ONE CAR: $2,500

BRIAN HUTCHINSON

I BOUGHT A CAR! Not just any car. My first car! Not the first car I ever had, mind you, but it was the first car I'd ever purchased. It was not a hand-me-down from the family. I bought it with my money. My scholarship money, but more on that later. It was my own; my precious! AND it was a maroon 1966 Mustang. There was only one problem … It was in North Carolina, and I was in Ohio.

I bought this car on eBay, you see. I had a supplemental scholarship that gave me a stipend for each semester's living expenses. It was supposed to be used for food, books, and stupid stuff like that, but a car meant a better job off-campus and a faster commute to the labs. Most importantly, I could leave the club at whatever time of night I wanted. FREEDOM! I was a younger man in those days, and it seemed like a good idea.

The description was perfect: "Cosmetic damage, needs work. The trunk lid is rusted, but I use it as my daily driver."

IT RAN!!!

That's all I needed to know. I chatted with the seller on the phone. He agreed to pick me up. Then we'd do an initial inspection of the car, and if all was well, he'd take me to the DMV to swap the title. If things weren't *kosher*, he'd take me back to the airport, and we'd go our separate ways. No hard feelings. However, unbeknownst to him, my mind was already made up. The Mustang was coming with me.

One-way ticket to North Carolina: $105

I had it all planned out. I printed out my MapQuest directions (yeah, that long ago) from Carolina to Columbus. I would get in at 9:00 a.m. The inspection and title would take about an hour and a half, maybe two hours. Then on the road by noon and back in Columbus right after sundown. The timing was crucial because I had an early morning lab the next day. I didn't tell anyone where I was going because it wouldn't even be for the whole day. Yeah, I was a younger man at the time.

The plane's wheels touched the ground right on time, and as soon as I got to the curb, here came my man. He was driving a beautifully restored early 70s pickup truck, just like he'd said. He had the build, beard, and hair color that made him look like a youngish Santa Claus, just like he'd said. And he was definitely a car guy, just like me.

We talked shop as we drove back to his house—carburetors and camshafts. It was a beautiful day in late October; there was not a cloud in the sky, and I couldn't think of a better setting in which to meet my new baby.

FINALLY! We pulled into his driveway and there it was. I spotted a dent on the left quarter panel. The paint on that side was faded and worn away (the cosmetic damage he described), but I already knew all that. I gave the exterior a cursory look, he handed me the keys, and I eased into the driver seat with reverence and anticipation. Insert key into ignition and turn ... *VROOM!* She started right up! The seller mentioned something about cleaning the windshields or shining the tires for me. No need for makeup, my man. I was already in love. Time to swap that title.

At around 12:30 p.m. we were back at his house. I pulled out of his driveway in my new 1966 Mustang Coupe. I'd be home in no time. All I had to do was get on ... get on ... Now I knew I should've been headed north. Let's check the directions. *Hmm* not in my backpack. Think back: What did you do this morning? Shower, breakfast, taxi. Shower, get dressed, breakfast, taxi. Shower, get dressed, breakfast, grab bag, taxi. Shower, get dressed, breakfast, grab bag, put snacks in bag, taxi ... Did you pick up the directions from the coffee table? No, they are still there!!!

DAMN IT!

No matter. The best-laid plans of mice and men, right? I would just go to a library and print some new ones. Easy peasy, lemon squeezy.

Two hours later I'd finally found a library. Thirty minutes after that (remember having to sign up for a computer? That long ago) I had my directions printed out.

Directions: 30 cents

It was now 3:00 p.m., and I was finally getting on the road. The route was simple. Take I-77 North, swoop through Virginia, then West Virginia into Ohio. Hook up with I-70 West and then … home. It was well past time to burn some rubber. Foot to the floor, I merged onto the highway. The engine roared, but the response was not immediate. The acceleration was slow at first, and I was about to put on my hazard lights, but the forty-year-old "auto-cruise" transmission kicked into the next gear and we were quickly approaching a respectable velocity. I noticed a vibration around 55 mph, but the car was almost 40 years old. You gotta let some stuff slide. However, we still had to make up some time … more power! The vibration smoothed out but at a little past 65, it returned to violently shaking! The entire car shook! It felt like an earthquake. I slowed down, and it stopped. Pulling the Mustang off to the side of the road, I jumped out and gave the car the best inspection I could at the moment. I checked the steering column, the shocks, the suspension, the planetary gears! I did everything except kick the tires. I couldn't find anything wrong so, back on the road, I went.

This time I watched carefully as we got up to speed. At 55 nothing happened. I cautiously approached 60. All good. 65 and the shaking was back! Before I could even slow down BOOM!!! Turns out, I should have kicked the tires because the left one had just exploded.

Fighting the wheel, I finally got pulled over to the left side of the road. There was nothing to be done. I needed a tow truck. I resigned myself to walking back to the last exit but not before retrieving my vintage 1966 Mustang hubcap from the middle of a four-lane highway. I was a younger man at the time.

The garage I found was, luckily enough, right on the exit. They towed me and gave me two front tires.

Tow and tires: $375

I was back on the road. It was 6:30 p.m., the sun was going down and I was still in North Carolina.

Virginia came and went without incident. There was a faint gasoline smell inside the car, so I opened the fresh air vents. Problem solved. We forged ahead, me and my Mustang.

Now cruising through the mountains of West Virginia around 10 p.m., and the temperature dropped considerably. It was time to close those vents. The smell was bad but not overpowering. It was certainly better than freezing. I turned the control knob. Nothing. Frosty mountain air continued to pour into the cabin. I tried again. Still no response. They were stuck in the open position, and I had neither the time nor tools to fix them. Pulling my sleeves over my fingers and gritting my teeth, I pressed on, determined to make it through these damned mountains.

It was a little while after that when I noticed, with teeth chattering, that I was low on gas. You see, forty years ago fuel efficiency was not a big concern. And a forty-year-old muscle car in the mountains of West Virginia guzzled faster than a frat boy during rush week. I could almost see the needle moving! And there was nothing outside of my windows. It was pitch black. There were no cities, no rest stops, no road signs. Nothing to signify I was anywhere near civilization. It was just me and my car. I passed up one dark exit after the next. I couldn't take the chance of roaming around in werewolf country.

I rode it out as long as I could, but eventually my hand was forced. Turning off on the next exit was one of the scariest things I had ever done. The off-ramp dead-ended at a road with one streetlight at the intersection. To the left was the tunnel under the highway and beyond that—nothingness. To the right, I could see the road went up a hill just before the light from the streetlamp failed. Beyond that, who knew? It was a coin flip.

"When in doubt … go right."

I turned the wheel and eased on the gas pedal. Me and my car were heading into the undiscovered country together. Right at the crest of the hill, the engine cut off. Now it was just me. There was a bend in the road, right at the end of the downhill. I figured I had enough momentum to get around that and then I'd have to decide what to do from there.

Despair was just starting to set in as I came around the turn, and all of a sudden the mighty "MOBILE" sign blazed forth in all its red, white, and blue glory! SALVATION! I coasted up to the gas pumps just ahead of a couple of guys pushing their Jeep. We all laughed as we recounted our stories of how we came to such lowly states. They wished me luck, and I like to think we would have hugged if they weren't so damn sweaty from pushing that Jeep.

Full gas tank: $23

The Mustang was alive again and we were in the home stretch. It was now 12:45 a.m.

Just a little before the Ohio state line I smelled what I thought was oil burning. I pulled over and checked the levels, but everything seemed okay. I bought a quart of 30 weight and poured half in just to be sure.

1 quart of oil: $11.92

At about 3:00 a.m. I was forty miles away from Columbus. Just outside of Pickerington, Ohio, I heard a loud POP, like a big firecracker. The steering was fine so, "NO, it was not the rear tires." We were, however, rapidly decelerating. I tried to get up to speed again, but she was not having it. There was a BANG this time, and I decided to stop at the next rest area.

When I popped the hood, it was immediately apparent what the problem was. The exhaust manifold was glowing cherry-red. The sound was backfire. I had pushed her too hard and the burning I had smelled earlier was probably what was left of the gaskets. I hunkered down and took a nap in the back while the 'Stang cooled down.

After twenty minutes or so, we took to the highway again. I put the hazard lights on, and we limped along at about 40 miles per hour.

About two blocks from my apartment, she finally gave out. I couldn't get the engine to turn over, and when I looked under the hood one more time, I saw the exhaust manifold had broken in two. She had done everything she could to get me home. I parked on a side street, grabbed my bag, and walked the rest of the way. When I opened the door, I could see the MapQuest directions on the table, openly mocking me. It was 5:00 a.m., and the sun was just lighting the morning sky. I slept.

When I woke up, I had some friends help me push Erica into my parking lot. If you're wondering why I named my car Erica, think of every Erica you know. You like them, but they're a little bitchy. We had many more adventures after that, Erica and me. I continued to pour money into fixing her, and she continued to break in new ways. Don't get me wrong. I loved that car. Just like any relationship, we had our ups and downs. My blood, sweat, and tears were literally in the car. Erica took me many places and left me stranded there. To paraphrase The Bard: "The evil that cars do lives after them." However, she did take me on what is still my greatest adventure. I sold her to a collector, used that money to move to New York City, and now I'm telling stories in front of you fine people.

Thank you, Erica, for helping a young man get his start, so long ago.

Total cost: I can never repay you.

36

MY GOD,
WHAT HAVE I DONE?

COLBY BLACK

I woke up with a pang of nostalgia. "Remember that time I drove a 35-year-old SUV that I bought on eBay across the country? Thank God I never have to do that again."

I rubbed my eyes, looked around, and reconnoitered.

Hmm.

Four thoughts crammed through my head at once. *Thought number 1*: This is not my beautiful apartment. *Thought number 2*: That is not my beautiful girlfriend. *Thought number 3*: There really is a large automobile parked outside.

In fact, I'm coming to in a hotel room in Walla Walla, Washington. This means this is still "that time" I drove a 35-year-old SUV that I'd bought on eBay across the country. Moreover, this being Walla Walla, Washington, it's only the second day of "that time" I drove a 35-year-old eBay purchase across the country. And there are at least six more days of "that time" I drove a 35-year-old SUV across the country.

Thought number 4: My God, what have I done?

Now, it's no accident that my thoughts are coagulating genuinely in the form of classic rock lyrics. If you've ever driven across this country, you know that the state of classic rock radio is alive and well. From left to right on your dial. From sea to shining sea.

So let's just walk through those four thoughts in order.

Thought number 1: This is not my beautiful apartment. At the time this story takes place, my beautiful apartment was in the middle of Manhattan.

Sure, they call it the "Upper" West Side. But look at the map. It's right in the middle of the island. Yes, I got that line from my apartment's leasing agent. And it is a line, but it's still a true statement. I'd been living in New York for almost five years after moving from Texas. Being from Texas means I am no stranger to road trips. They were natured and nurtured into me.

I come from a family of gear heads. I had an uncle that rebuilt a Model T. Another uncle used to have this sweet orange 1972 Ford pickup he inherited from my grandfather. A third uncle owns a body shop and a pristine 1957 Thunderbird. He once charged my dad $50 to take a dent out of our car. My dad was expecting it to be free. My uncle thought otherwise and said, "You better charge your friends because your enemies won't do business with you."

That stuck with me.

It also stuck with my dad, who has brought it up just enough to get his $50 worth out of that experience.

If I had to say my parents have a hobby, it's driving, and every summer they'd load up the Buick and drive us to LA ... at precisely 55 miles an hour the whole 1,067-mile way. I was born and raised in an area of the Texas Panhandle so remote and desolate, we had to drive an hour just to get to the nearest movie theater. A high school football game in our district meant someone was spending six hours of their Friday on a yellow school bus.

Thought number 2: That is not my beautiful girlfriend. I am not sharing this hotel room in Walla Walla, Washington with my girlfriend, Jess. I am also not alone.

Sadly, I am sharing my hotel room with one of the top five ranked snorers in the New World. Todd Van Horne is my own best frenemy.

I'm not sure how to say this, but Todd is—SIMULTANEOUSLY, in absolutely every single instant—the very first and the very last person you want with you on an interstate road trip. Todd's sense of direction is like a homing pigeon crossed with a monarch butterfly. It's remarkable. Equally remarkable is his desire to get off the interstate and "see what's out there," like the proverbial cat of curiosity. He pulled this once on a trip to Ohio. We got off the interstate to "see what's out there" and found ourselves on a two-lane road behind an Amish buggy for 20 minutes. We topped out at about 11 miles an hour before "Slow Ride" came on the radio. Which you'd think would have made the event stick with me and sink in. It did not.

So, on this latest endeavor Todd was copiloting and noticed we were just an inch on the map from Oregon's Crater Lake. Now, the trouble was, if you were willing to zoom waaaay out, you were only an inch on the map from just about anywhere. (We are, at present, in this very room in Manhattan's East Village, an inch from Atlanta.) Todd and I had both heard a bit about Crater Lake and neither of us had ever been there. And, again, it was only an inch on the map from us.

Crater Lake sits in a perfect bowl formed when a volcano blew its top. There are no rivers or streams flowing into it or out of it. It's the cleanest body of water in North America. It's also completely shielded from the wind by the lip of the mountain. There is nary a ripple on its surface. Crater Lake is legitimately mind-blowing.

Todd and I walked, nay, we strutted, around Crater Lake for an hour or so like we had done something. Like we had discovered this place.

I promise you it's something you should visit once.

Please, visit it once.

Please, visit it only once.

Although only an inch away on the map, it added 12 hours of driving to Day One. Even in April, many of the roads were still closed from snow, which forced one (or, in this case, me) to drive up and around the rim of the mountain and then back around and down said mountain. Do I need to mention that, after I white-knuckled the steering wheel back down the mountain while riding the brakes and legitimately stress sweating, Todd had the nerve to say, "That detour wasn't that bad?"

Perhaps what kept me from killing Todd that day was the impact it would have on my relationship with my girlfriend. Jess is an actual, for real Jersey girl. She pumps her fist. She gives directions with exit numbers in them. Jess says "Austin, Texas," and I wonder if that is near "Austin, Texas." I told you—she's a for real Jersey Girl.

I was too old and grizzled to believe in love at first sight, but the first time I saw her I was head over heels. So, of course, that meant there was a rapid uptick in my time in Jersey. I hadn't seen this coming and it caused Jess to worry about my sanity.

However, not for the reasons you think. She worried about my sanity because while it was ridiculously easy for me to get into and out of her place from the city, I was kinda stuck once I was there. There was not much within walking distance and cycling seemed a bit dodgy.

Thought number 3: There really is a large automobile parked outside. About a week or so after we brought this up, we were at dinner with some of her friends. A couple of us guys decided we all needed to live next to each other.

With basements.

That we could connect with a tunnel system.

We kept drinking.

Even dumber ideas came out. One of the guys mentioned that he always wanted an old Jeep CJ. I said I always wanted an old Landcruiser or Defender, but they always seemed pretty expensive for their age.

"It seems like you can find some great deals on old International Scouts, though."

Even though those words came out of my mouth, it took me about half an hour to pair my obvious need with my obvious opportunity.

I didn't need a daily driver. Didn't care about fuel economy or reliability. I didn't want to spend much money and didn't want a giant insurance liability. I didn't want something that looked like it should be stolen or might hold anything valuable.

So, impractical, gas-guzzling, unreliable, cheap, worthless. Pretty sure you Google those things, and the International Scout comes up. But I'll just guess you have no idea what an International Scout is. The International Harvester Company was founded in 1902 when John Pierpont Morgan merged five agricultural manufacturing companies. They made tractors. They made trucks. And, in 1958, their head of engineering tasked his minions with designing "something to replace the horse."

Horses, as you may be aware, had an evolutionary head start of millions of years. Somehow, 24 months later, trusty steeds all over America were replaced by the Scout, from International.

As you might expect, when a tractor company made an SUV, they weren't exactly stylish hot rods, but you could probably tow a house with them. They also featured four-wheel drive systems that could best anything General Motors and Ford had a decade later. However, this plan of International's had a few problems. Chiefly, they had no dealership network for these things. They had no good way to sell their new SUVs, which led to also having no good way to service them. In fact, many Scouts were given away for free to farmers who had bought a new International Harvester tractor.

They weren't exactly coveted machines at the time, which was to say they were never really coveted machines. Most of them weren't babied. Oh, they also had an amazing proclivity to start rusting almost immediately. International Scouts were more likely to roll over than a dog named Scout.

It might surprise you to learn that, in 1980, International found the Scout to be a bad business decision and stopped production. No one noticed. Horses all over America came out of retirement.

Despite this plan's merits, I remained unconvinced that Jess could possibly think this hair-brained scheme conceived on alcohol was a good idea. One random Tuesday, I blurted out,

"Oh. I bought a Scout today."

"You did! That's awesome. Tell me about it."

Okay, I hadn't. That was a test. A dry run to see how she really felt about all this nonsense. It seemed she didn't think it was nonsense. She thought I should ... like ... I don't know ... Do things that make me happy or some such.

Thought number 4: My God, what have I done?

Well, shit.

I had a track record of women thinking my hair-brained ideas were hair-brained ideas. I mean ... they were hair-brained ideas. And I grew accustomed to the pushback. It kept me honest. And stagnant.

And resentful. Honestly stagnant resentfulness. That was my sweet spot.

That was my 20s.

And early 30s.

And mid-30s.

Oh shit! This Jess girl wasn't going to think my wild, wacky ideas were wild, wacky ideas. Truth be told, I wasn't some amazing optimist. I just kept getting up after every knockdown. There were a lot of knockdowns. Still, there are few things more terrifying and exhilarating than having a best frenemy and a girlfriend who encourages and supports your hair-brained ideas that seem to be a culmination of your entire upbringing and life.

In fact, I can think of only two things more terrifying and exhilarating than that. One of them is when you're watching the clock tick down on an eBay auction for a 1978 International Scout, and you're the high bidder.

The second thing is five minutes after the auction closes, and you've won, and you look down and say, "Oh. Shit. This thing's in fucking Rogue River, Oregon. Where the hell is that?"

I wrote down three goals for the trip: 1. Get to Oregon. 2. Get back to New York. 3. Don't kill Todd. The third was mostly optional, but all three were accomplished. After finally hearing every classic rock song ever recorded, we wheeled into Jess's place in New Jersey at about 4:00 a.m. on a Sunday morning. The sun came through the window, and I woke up a very few, very short hours later and felt an immense sense of relief and joy and accomplishment.

We really had done it. We really had driven a 35-year-old International Scout named Jolene across the country that I'd bought on eBay sight unseen. It was real.

And this time we really never had to do it again.

This is my beautiful girlfriend. This is her beautiful apartment. Once in a lifetime.

Molly Touger | "In Transit" Storyteller

When I started to write my *No, YOU Tell It!* story, I had to make a choice: Whether to hint from the beginning that the terrible thing that happens turns out not to be so terrible. Or take the audience through the experience as I lived it.

I chose the latter.

When I was 12, for part of an afternoon, I thought my dad was dead. And then I found what had died was a hamster.

It's funny but not funny. On account of the hamster. On account of the fact that I really thought my dad was dead.

One of the most unique things about the *No, YOU Tell It!* experience is getting to watch the audience react to what you've written. You sit onstage while your story-swap partner reads. It's about as close to an out-of-body experience as you can get.

It started out lovely. I watched while Rebecca presented my awkward, persnickety 12-year-old self to the audience. I could see them commiserate and relate. I could enjoy the benefits of self-revelation without having to bare my soul personally.

But then she read the part where my dad "dies." I watched their faces fall. Even listening to the recording now I can feel the abrupt shift to heaviness. It lasts for 3 ½ minutes.

I remember sitting on stage and wondering if my choice had been the right one. If I should have included the information upfront that my dad was currently okay. If I should lean forward and whisper, "*It turns out fine!*"

But I didn't. I committed to the story that I'd written. I let Rebecca tell it.

When Rebecca made the big reveal, the room blew up with laughter. Daddy hadn't died. Teddy had. I was pleased. We'd led them through the darkness and back into the light.

Except that I found out afterward that at least one person didn't enjoy the journey. They were triggered because of their own experience with loss. They had identified and then felt manipulated when the death in my story turned out not to be as it seemed.

And then I read the story to another friend months after the performance and she started crying during the part where I thought my dad was dead and I hadn't said goodbye. It turned out she'd had a recent, similar trauma.

I've thought about these reactions a lot over the years. And especially recently. Because this past year my dad did actually die. And, of course, it wasn't funny at all.

The death wasn't sudden like in the story, but the diagnosis was. It made me understand the phrase "the moment when everything changes." There was the before when my family was safe and whole. There was the moment it got hit by a freight train. And there were a million moments after where we broke piece by piece.

It made me realize a few things.

For a long time, I worried I'd made the wrong choice. That by not sharing upfront that the dearly departed was a hamster, that maybe I'd appropriated the experience of shock and loss.

I now know I didn't appropriate. While it lasted, the "hit by a train" moment was real.

But I also know that if now-me was listening to then-me tell that story, during the "thought he was dead" part, I would be hysterical. Now-me knows profound loss. Now-me sometimes drowns in the "after" moments.

On the other hand, if now-me were to tell the story, it would be a different story. I'd probably start with something like: "The first time my dad died, he didn't." I might land on the point about how lucky I'd gotten when I was 12—that I got to have what everyone wishes for when something terrible happens. For it to be a mistake and for everything to go back to the way it was.

But that's the thing about stories. As you change, so do they. You just never know which direction things will go.

Part of what makes the *No, YOU Tell It!* experience so special, is that when you write your story—committing to the truth and telling it as best you understand it at that moment—you get to see it refracted. You see something different when you hear what your paired storyteller emphasizes. You see something different as the director shapes the telling. And you see something different yet again when you see a room full of people react in real-time.

I think about that 3 ½ minutes of silence and the subsequent reactions. I realize now those feedback points were prescient. They were telling me a larger truth I didn't yet know.

SEEYOUINTHEMORNINGILOVEYOUGOODNIGHT.

MOLLY TOUGER

That's how we say it in my family. One word. Like *Supercalafragelistic*. Or *Fugheddaboudit*. I have no idea how it started, but when I was a kid, I insisted upon it. Once tucked in, I would say it: *Seeyouinthemorningcloveyougoodnight*. And then my mom or dad had to say it back: *Seeyouinthemorningcloveyougoodnight*. My parents thought it more sweet than OCD and, in fact, we still say it when I go home to visit. I don't insist on it anymore — which is good because I'm 37. But, truth be told, I prefer to say it than not.

As a kid, I was into rituals. In addition to *Seeyouinthemorningcloveyougoodnight* every evening, I'd set up a pair of shoes by my bed, heels together, toes out, because I'd learned from *Reading Rainbow* that this would keep evil spirits away. When I woke up, I would go straight to the piano to play the right-hand part of Mouret's *Rondeau* — the opening theme of *Masterpiece Theater*. A perfect run was a good omen. As you can see, PBS had a strong influence on me. It was all that my parents watched and one of the few channels that came in on our crappy black-and-white television.

My rituals, like most rituals, were an attempt to control forces beyond me, an appeal for well-being. Once I got to school everything was out of my hands. I was skinny, shy, prone to getting lost in my own thoughts, and constantly setting off social tripwires. If I wasn't saying the wrong thing, I was bringing the wrong lunch or wearing the wrong ski jacket. Since I couldn't predict when I'd screw up, I tried to blend into the wall. Invisibility equaled peace.

As a young kid, I blamed myself for my inability to fit in. Clearly, I was just inherently flawed. But over time it dawned on me that it was actually my parents' fault. Who put a lamb chop wrapped in wax paper in my lunch bag? Who bought the off-brand ski jacket at the Bargain Center? Who left New York to plop our Jewish, olive-skinned family in a town full of white pasty Irish Catholics, simply so my dad could be a professor? Toward the end of elementary school, I sometimes fantasized my parents would die, forcing me to live with their friends in California who had an in-ground pool and three kids who each had their own TVs. They would buy me a Nintendo and a full wardrobe of Esprit clothing. I could start over in a place where my reputation was not indelibly set as "the weird girl."

By the time I was 13, I was fully irascible but significantly less isolated. I had developed a close group of girlfriends, and while neither cool nor terribly popular, I was no longer a constant target. I spent the summer of 1988 working as a junior camp counselor at a day camp, leading six-year-olds in choruses of *Boom-Chikka-Boom*, and nights and weekends out with my girlfriends. As we were good girls, "out" generally meant the mall, the movies, or someone's house making Rice Krispie treats. But that was okay. If I was home, I was lame. If I was out, I was all right.

It was in the middle of that summer that my dad went to a Physics conference in Pittsburgh. We often tacked our family vacations on to his conferences—frequently to places I didn't want to go, like Bozeman, Montana. But because it was Pittsburgh, this year the family vacation part had gotten nixed.

The night before he left, my dad knocked on my bedroom door and stuck his head in. "*Seeyouinthemorningkloveyougoodnight!*" he said cheerily.

"Dad, you need to wait for me to say, 'Come in.'" He closed the door and this time knocked. This irritated me more. "Just come in," I said. He opened the door.

"I'm leaving early, so I'm going to say goodbye now," he said.

"Say goodbye in the morning."

"You *really* want me to wake you up?" The dubiousness was fair; the next day was Sunday and most weekends I slept until noon.

"No," I said still staring at my book. "I'll get up on my own." As he closed the door, it was on the tip of my tongue: *Seeyouinthe-morningkloveyougoodnight.* But because I was annoyed, I didn't say it.

When I woke up at noon, he was gone. I felt a pang of guilt but forgot it when Marie called to ask if I wanted to watch *Top Gun* in her basement with our other friends. Marie O'Neal was my best friend; her basement was our regular summer hangout because it had air conditioning, an orange shag rug for lounging, and an excellent selection of snacks.

It was early evening, and we were sprawled and stuffing ourselves with Cool Ranch Doritos when Mrs. O'Neal yelled down to say that my mom was on the phone. Annoyed at being forced to move, I hauled myself off the carpet and trudged upstairs.

I picked up the receiver. "Yup?"

"Your sister won't go to bed until she tells you something," my mom said.

My sister was 7 and stubborn, so this didn't surprise me.

"Fine," I said. "Put her on."

My sister got on and immediately I could tell she'd been crying.

"What's wrong?" I said, not entirely sympathetically. At the time she fell into the category of wrongs-done-me-by-my-family; she was more popular and sportier than I had been at her age, and her cheery existence dented my theory that our parents ruined lives.

She sobbed and didn't answer.

"What's wrong?" I said again.

She said something I couldn't understand: *"Da-ee eye,"* she sniffed.

"What?" I said.

"Da-ee eye!"

And suddenly I got it: *Daddy died.*

"What?" I whispered. There was shuffling as she handed the phone back to my mother. I braced myself against the hall table.

"Is it true?" I asked.

"I'm afraid so," my mother said. She sounded almost nonchalant.

"Can you come get me?"

"Aren't the O'Neals driving you home?"

"Can you come get me?" I said again, and perhaps hearing my distress, my mother agreed.

"Well ... all right. I'll be there in 20 minutes."

I hung up the phone and stood for a moment. Then I opened the basement door, walked down a few steps, and sat down on the stairs.

Below me, my friends were lazing where I'd left them. On TV, Maverick and Goose were getting reamed out by their commanding officer for flying below 10,000 feet. It was quiet except for the TV and the crunching of Doritos. I tried to think of what I was supposed to do. My thoughts were like vapor. They formed and disappeared. I sat with my hands in my lap. Eventually someone looked up. "Are you okay?"

"My dad died," I said.

Suddenly they were running up the stairs, hugging me, asking me what happened. I didn't know. Marie ran to tell her parents. I felt numb. Then there was the sound of a stampede; Marie's parents had been told. Arms hauled me into the dining room and placed me in a chair. Marie's mom kept her hands on my shoulders.

"Honey, what happened?" she asked. I said again that I didn't know—it hadn't occurred to me to find out. Maybe the plane went down. Maybe it was a heart attack. I could see my friends crying but couldn't hear them. It was as if someone had turned the volume down and there was only the one thought repeating: *Daddy died.* I hadn't said goodbye.

"Can I get you some water?" Marie's mom asked. I shook my head. Everyone stared at me. I stared at a spot in the middle of the table and tried to make myself feel something. *Daddy died.* My dad who went birdwatching in the neighborhood with binoculars, making me terrified that people would think he was a peeping Tom. My dad, who drew my birth announcement, showing my parents as cartoon chickens welcoming an egg. My dad who filled every shelf in our house with antique books from garage sales, who planned all our vacations, who smelled like Old Spice when he'd kiss me goodnight after he and my mom went on dates. Would we still go on vacation? Would we move? Would my mom marry someone else?

After a few minutes, Marie's mom asked if I wanted to lie down on the couch. I shook my head again and then suddenly, like vomit coming up, adrenaline flooded my body. I got up and ran to the front door and outside. Everyone chased after me. I got to the middle of the yard and Marie's dad grabbed me and hugged me tight. I sobbed and my knees buckled. I could barely breathe.

It was then that my mother's white Honda Civic materialized at the corner. She pulled into the driveway, her window down. She looked surprisingly cheerful for a new widow.

Marie's mom walked up to the car.

"Hallie, I'm so sorry," she said. "What was it?"

"A hamster," my mom said. And there it was. A hamster had killed my father. For a moment I imagined it must have been like the story where the mouse kills the elephant by climbing up his trunk. A hamster on the plane. It had climbed up my dad's nose, out of his plastic cup, and suffocated him.

"Excuse me?" said Mrs. O'Neal.

"Naomi's hamster died," my mom said, looking increasingly confused, having now taken in the group of weeping eighth-grade girls and her prostrate daughter.

"*Teddy* died?" I said, still clinging to Mr. O'Neal.

"Oh my God, we thought Jerry died!" Mrs. O'Neal said, comprehending the mistake in identity. Then she began to laugh. And then everyone else laughed. I didn't. The adrenaline was shifting from grief to humiliation and fury.

"I thought you said Daddy died," I whispered.

"He's in Pittsburgh," my mom said. "He called earlier. He's fine."

"How could you let me think he was dead?" I yelled.

"How could I know what you thought?" my mother said reasonably, which infuriated me more.

Fully relieved now, my friends were wracked with fits of giggles, Mr. O'Neal doubled over, wiping his twinkly Irish eyes.

"*Teddy died!*" he cried.

My cheeks burned.

"Do you still want to come home?" my mom said.

"Yes," I said. I didn't understand how this could suddenly be hilarious. I had thought my father was dead. That wasn't funny. I wanted to be alone.

I got in the car, and we drove home. I asked if I could skip camp the next day. My mother said no.

I don't remember my dad coming home, save that by the time he'd arrived I'd gotten over his being dead. I quickly resumed resenting both of my parents.

But *SeeyouinthemorningIloveyougoodnight*—I never *didn't* say it again. Just in case.

SONG LINES

REBECCA HART

I. Song Lines

A Songline also called a dreaming track by <u>Indigenous Australians</u>, is a path across the land <...> followed by 'creator-beings' during the DreamTime (i.e., Creation). The paths of the songlines are recorded in traditional songs <...>. The songs must be continually sung to keep the land "alive." —*Wikipedia*

"Those who ancient lines did ley/Will heed the song that calls them back" —*Jethro Tull*

II. A Song's Lines

Kyrie
Sanctify
Never more be
you have heard the tale
one hundred times before me
when the nighttime comes
and the salt wind blows
then the mother ship comes sailing
on the white sea foam
do not hide your heart
do not break your hold
when the mother ship may call you
you will surely go

These are the lyrics to a song. It is a song in the style of a certain kind of ballad that comes to us from (usually) Ireland, that talks about another world, the faery world. The songs describe this place as beautiful but dangerous ... since anyone who goes there will find themselves unable to return.

This song is like that. Except it was written by me, in college. I recorded that song—you can get it online I think—but I didn't play it "out" much. Or at all. It was never the right place or the right time.

III. Dreamtime

When I first visited Ireland, I was 12 years old, and my father had decided it was time to take us (my mother, my sister, and me) there for some time with the ancestors (on his side). We touched down at Shannon airport; I looked out the window at the green hills and heard myself think, with unshakable certainty:

Oh, I'm home.

Now, that wasn't true. I was born in New York, raised in New Jersey, and am an American citizen. And yet...

From that moment, Ireland's non-literal landscape was never far from me—my dreams, my music, or my general aesthetic—though I didn't see the country again until I was in college. To the bewilderment of friends and family, I chose to do my semester abroad in "Ireland's Texas" (not my joke), County Cork. Perhaps traumatized by the dissonance of Real World: University College Cork vs. the Fantasy Mother Ship Ireland of my childhood, I didn't visit again for ten years.

In 2005, I found myself in Dublin for a long weekend with a boyfriend who was not my boyfriend for much longer after that trip. It had been a long time coming but it was, of course, Ireland that finally broke us up. Watching his response, or lack of such, to the country, I realized he did not and would not ever really understand me. (Fair? Who knows? But it's always been that way.) In my life, Ireland calls the shots. She is my life, my love, and my lady. (Brandy, you're a fine girl, et cetera.)

On the last night of that trip, we were at a pub with my Dublin Theatre Friend Sharon and a few others. Sharon was urging me to come for a longer visit and to stay.

"You know, you should really come in the Fall when the Theatre Festivals are happening. You've that one-woman show you wrote.

You could maybe do it over here, or at least meet some heads, you know, theatre heads, who could talk to you about it. It's really best if you're here, not emailing, you know."

I answered Sharon with kind of a sad shrug, saying, "Yeah, I'd love to, but you know I have this day job, and I really can't get the time off…"

…then the mother ship comes sailing
on the white sea foam…

A few months later an email from her, addressed to me and another woman. "Mary, meet Rebecca. Rebecca, meet Mary. Mary is looking for someone to swap apartments with, New York-to-Dublin, in September/October, during the time of the theatre festivals."

(I could hear the emphasis on those last few words.)

…when the mother ship may call you
You will surely go

Before you could say "Ancestral Homeland," I had divested myself of both day job and boyfriend, booked a scarily low number of gigs (I think three, which turned into fourteen JUST before I got there because the Irish are more, shall we say, spontaneous in their business dealings), and a plane ticket. Sharon had also set up a meeting with a literary manager from the famed Druid Theatre who had agreed to host a reading of my solo show. With that good news, I was away.

IV. Kyrie, Sanctify

"My house," I email giddily to my sister over my cup of Barry's Tea, "has a blue door and a black gate. I love it."

A month ago, a long black cast-iron key (I kid you not) arrived in a padded envelope in my NY mailbox, and now I'm here. Mary's place is in a suburb of Dublin called Drimnagh. It has a backyard where a magpie and a gray cat hang out, and—miracle of NY miracles—TWO FLOORS. An upstairs AND a downstairs. It's also a block from the LUAS, the brand-spanking-new above-ground transit system that speaks the names of each stop in both English and Irish, using soothing automated tones. (Drimnagh, if you're wondering, sounds pretty much the same in both.)

"Drimnagh. *Drimnagh.*"

I'm getting pretty good at my pronunciation.

"Goldenbridge. *An Droichead Orga.*"

I've also managed to settle into touring in Ireland as if I've been doing it all my life instead of two weeks. I have a routine: Get on a cross-country train (you can get cross country in three hours, so I've already done it several times). Lunch from the train snack cart that comes around. Get to the venue, or the pub. Sound check. Pint. Play. Listen. Make new friends.

In Wexford, the owner of the venue insisted on one of my CDs in lieu of payment for my night in the hotel (which he also owned). In Dundalk, the radio DJ insisted I come back home with him to meet the wife and have a spot of lunch. I never want to leave. *She met the host one night on a moonlit cobblestone street and was never heard from again.*

Do not hide your heart
Do not break your hold…

Yesterday I stood on the train platform in Galway thinking, "How did I afford this train ticket?" Then I remembered I'd been getting paid to play. Talk about culture shock.

When the mother ship may call you…

It's dusk. I put my teacup in the sink, slide on my leather jacket, rumple my boy-cut hair, and pick up my guitar. I have a gig "in town" tonight, at the Project Arts Centre in Dublin's Temple Bar.

V. Hallelujah

Sometimes, a gig is just a gig. This is not one of those times.

Tonight, I already know things will be different. The Project Arts Centre is not a pub or a music venue, but a Theatre. Not just a Theatre but a Very Hip Experimental Contemporary Theatre. And not just a Very Hip Experimental Contemporary Theatre, either, but—since, again, Ireland is very small—THE Very Hip Experimental Modern Contemporary Theatre. That there is. In the country.

It's like, ok, pretend New York Theatre Workshop and St Ann's Warehouse and, I don't know, BAM, were all just rolled into one cube-shaped black-boxy type space and funded by the City Arts Council. Pretend there's an Arts Council, for that matter. And pretend that because of a general confidence in their audience, the theatre is able and willing to put up a run of shows with no set script and no consistent cast. Shows fluid enough in nature to, say, cast a complete stranger in, the day before, without fanfare beyond: "Why don't you come along tomorrow night and play a few songs in the show?"

In case you haven't figured it out, that stranger was me.

A week ago I'd had a meeting with the Artistic Director of the Project Arts about my solo show. He was a lovely man who somehow made me completely forget he was an Important Theatre Person and I was a Shaggy Interloper. He congratulated me for having my show staged in Galway but was clear that the piece was of no interest to St. BAM's Theatre Workshop of Temple Bar. However, before sending me into the gray afternoon, he made the above offer, and I—jacked up on good will and chocolate biscuits—agreed.

I didn't learn much about the actual "show" that I was going to be "in," only that the theme was Dublin itself—the city's history, people, and culture—and yet, somehow, it was going to involve me.

"I don't really have any songs about Ireland," I'd said. They said that was *Grand*.

Upon arrival I find that the program, besides me, features a couple of Irish actors reading selections from James Joyce's *Ulysses* and a charming elderly Dublin historian who lectured about Dublin fun facts.

I know!! Can you imagine anything more exciting? Or more commercially viable by usual standards?

But it's great.

The audience—the full house of who are these people???!!!— applaud enthusiastically. They applaud my songs! They applaud after the James Joyce readings. They applaud after Dublin Historian drones on about … something … for like twenty minutes.

I do, too. The whole thing is just kind of beautiful and pleasant if somewhat disorganized and kind of (ssh) boring. But it's happening. It's okay. No one is going to Show Business Jail. And everyone is listening.

Then, something unexpected happens.

Dublin Historian starts gently telling everyone to get up on their feet for the last portion of the evening. They do. The doors behind me in the back wall of the theatre (there's a door there?) are being opened. The streetlamp, and the breeze from the River Liffey, floods in. We can hear the lads in Temple Bar shouting, acoustic guitar covers, the occasional horn honking—Dublin of an evening. The cobblestones are wet. It's raining softly, but that's not unusual, and no one seems to care much.

We all exit the theatre and follow the white-headed historian out into the night. He doesn't say where we're going, and no one asks. No one tells me I have to go too, but I follow. Also, no one tells me to take my guitar with me—I've played my two songs already—but I do.

When the nighttime comes
And the salt wind blows…

Umbrellas go up, and we all walk close together in a sort of merry hush, with purpose, all somehow now in the show. Our guide leads us around a corner and down into an alley.

It's dark now, fully night. No streetlights, just the brilliant moon lighting everything from the raindrops on the grass to the sudden, freestanding, incongruous black iron gate someone opens and we all—silently now—pass through.

We all huddle together on a little plot of grass between two buildings, hidden from the street and from the world. All the sounds of the city fall away. It's still raining, a "soft rain," gentle on your skin. The umbrellas stay up. The faces around me are a kindly blur as our guide introduces us to this secret spot. It's special. I know that it is before he even says anything. I feel a hum in the air, a swimming behind my eyes. Something stirs and locks beneath my feet, rooting me to the spot. I stand very still, waiting. For something.

"This, ladies and gentlemen," he says, "is the very place where Handel's 'Messiah,' with its wonderful 'Hallelujah Chorus,' was performed for the very first time. The first time in the world, right here."

An appreciative murmuring. I know what's coming next before he says it.

"And, ladies and gentlemen, as far as we know, there hasn't been any music performed on this spot at all … until now."

He points at me. Everyone turns to look. And I realize I didn't bring my guitar with me to this moment; it brought me. And I also suddenly remember a song. A song for this time, and this place; a place I have never, actually, left. And, standing under the black umbrellas, among the smiling faces of the Host, I play it. I sing the place alive, as it will be again, and as it has been before,

Kyrie,

Sanctify,

one hundred times before me.

LEGACY

June 8th, 2014
The Brick | Brooklyn

Podcast Episode 68

"League of Absence"
written by E. James Ford
and performed by Nicole Greevy

"Nerd: The Next Generation"
written by Nicole Greevy
and performed by E. James Ford

Legacy Artwork: Sha-Née Williams

Erika Iverson | Director and Founding Member

As part of our second anniversary, *No, YOU Tell It!* participated in The Brick's Comic Book Theater Festival in Brooklyn. For this show, we tried something inspired by the festival's exploration of the "intersection of the live and the drawn, the ink and the actor." Usually we give our storytellers a theme to inspire their true tales with plenty of room for multiple interpretations. This time, we only provided the "Legacy" theme to comic artist Sha-Née Williams and asked her to interpret it into a visual prompt.

Sha-Née created a composite image of two Black female superheroes—one large, front-facing portrait of a woman looking over a city and one action pose with a younger-looking woman running to the rescue. We gave this image to our four storytellers without the word "Legacy" or any further context. After they completed their first drafts, Sha-Née joined our story meetings and drew unique illustrations for each of their true tales. In spite of the fact that we didn't share the theme, our storytellers ended up writing about the personal legacies we leave behind.

Perhaps because of the subtle generational themes in Sha-Née's initial illustration, they each brought in narratives about the powerful imaginations of children. E. James Ford's story begins with a letter of resignation from an imaginary group of superheroes, while Nicole Greevy ponders the small family crisis brought on when her son wants to dress up as Wonder Woman. Sha-Née later admitted that her biggest challenge for the commissioned illustrations was drawing kids, which were not her usual subjects in comic book art. One panel shows a childhood version of E. James and his friends with robot feet and glowing magic rings. The other, a memorable masterpiece, depicts Nicole as Wonder Woman, holding her child's hand as he proudly sports his felt tiara.

These are some of my favorite stories from this early period of *No, YOU Tell It!* I like them because they are sneaky. You think you understand where they are going, then suddenly, they pull a left turn, revealing themselves to be weird stories about whether it is okay to be weird. The act of storytelling is one of remembering, and "Legacy" asks how we are willing to be remembered. Whether it's Nicole Greevy's description of her husband wearing his mother's dress or E. James Ford announcing his membership in the Superhero League of "Tap-and-Jazz Class," each story says something about the reluctance to know ourselves, to believe in something strange, to announce yourself or let your child announce themselves as "different."

These stories ask us: What are the limits on what is okay to imagine? Who sets those limits for us? It's easy to blame a parent for nixing a gender-specific superhero costume, but when do we become the police of our own imaginations?

I still go back and listen to the podcast featuring these stories every once in a while, and I've recommended the episode to people who want to learn about *No, YOU Tell It!* I'm personally affected by these stories. I tear up a little when I hear the "League of Absence" narrator admit that he ducks out the door before the magic leaves a project or a love affair. I still get goose pimples when "Nerd: The Next Generation" imagines the prom of the future, where kids will feel free to wear whatever they want, in every shape and silhouette imaginable. Perhaps one day we will all feel free enough to dress like superheroes.

LEAGUE OF ABSENCE

E. JAMES FORD

Citizens of Earth and Members of the Guardian Mutant League:

Since arriving on your planet, I have been a dues-paying member of several of your superhero leagues. With my comrades-in-arms, I have battled giant kaiju ro-beasts, deactivated satellite death beams that threatened to destroy the planet, and ventured through inter-dimensional portals to defeat an evil version of myself that wanted to become the overlord of a small section of South Brooklyn. I also have extensive experience writing press releases, developing cross-channel marketing strategies, and in event planning. I believe my experience speaks for itself.

My league membership covers a wide range of fields, from golden-age liberty teams to vigilante street justice squads to 1970s psychedelic hero guilds. Some of the more prominent leagues of which I've been a member include the Mighty Rebels, the Trench Coat Avengers, the Justice Force, the Squad Force, the Street Force, the Force Squad, MegaTeam USA, Tap-and-Jazz Class, The League of Extraordinary Stoners, the Dallas Rocky Horror Picture Show cast, SuperMercenaries, NeckPunchers, and, of course, this one here. With all of you.

I would like to formally tender my resignation.

I feel it's best to do so now before things get weird. Before we stop being heroes and transform into regular folks loitering on the sidewalk trying to decide where to get a drink. As things stand now in this small room, we are ostensibly perched atop a national monument with trumpets swelling in the major chords of vanquished enemies. But we both know what happens next after the credits roll: We'll realize the music sounds a little hackneyed; that the monument we're perched on is *more* than a little phallic; and the triumph of our actions can't withstand the analysis of moral-relativism in a cultural context.

I learned long ago that no superhero, no matter how great his or her powers, can hope to withstand the dreadful force that has been destroying our kind since time immemorial. Self-awareness, with its awesome power, can vanquish the most noble acts in the blink of an eye and will send most supers cowering to their secret lairs or, even worse, into middle-management positions.

I first encountered this psychic kryptonite in the very first superhero league that I ever joined. I was in grade school, and the league was formed in the rush of morning recesses and the 30 minutes after school we spent waiting for our parents to pick us up.

That's one of the things about us supers—we always seem to find each other. It's that unmistakable feeling when you lock eyes with another one of your kind and realize there is a magic you both can do, energy beams and anti-gravity waves reverberating beneath both of your fingertips. It's how I felt when I first saw all of you. It was irresistible and I knew that, together, we could save this city from itself.

Back in second grade, there were four of us. Four superheroes concentrated in one hippy-dippy town just outside of Salt Lake City, Utah. None of us were Mormon, before you ask. In fact, I don't think there are very many Mormon superheroes. It has nothing to do with their system of belief ... There are plenty of superheroes who believe in some crazy stuff (Green Lantern, I'm looking at you). It's just that most superheroes smoke, and the Mormons have a thing about smoking so it makes being a superhero rather complicated.

We discovered our powers during a sleepover in my family's basement. Unbeknownst to my unsuspecting parents, the house was being attacked from all sides by the ghosts from the video game Pac-Man (trademark). An ambiguous evil wizard had made the ghosts invisible, so my parents couldn't see them. No, only those with superpowers like ours could see where they attacked from. Our special abilities manifested out of nowhere, the way they often do, just as the ghosts burst through the door and sprayed the basement with machine-gun fire. Yes, these ghosts had machine guns.

Standing back-to-back, we faced the menacing specters. I would ensnare the ghosts in a net of multi-colored energy beams that launched from a ring made of moonrock, while Jennie and Chad fired lasers from their hands and eyes, which disintegrated the ghosts into piles of ash. Benji was on shields, protecting us in a globe of transparent anti-matter that stopped the ghosts' bullets from piercing our skin.

We were unstoppable. A bond was formed and from that day forward, we fought and vanquished many foes and thwarted many disasters large and small. Our secret base was on a spaceship, hovering just above Earth's atmosphere. Connected to the ship were four invisible elevator shafts that led directly from all of our houses to the command bridge. In the event of an alien attack or some other world crisis, we could be ready-for-action in seconds.

Like many superhero leagues of the time, we also had a side music project: A hard-rock band that did covers of songs by The Monkees. I am aware this might sound weird to some of you younger supers, but it was the Eighties. Most of the great superhero leagues at the time were in also rock bands. Galaxy Rangers. Kidd Video. Look it up. It was just what you did.

Through all of our adventures, we could never shake the menace of those ghosts who attacked us on the first night. Somehow, whether we were battling werewolves or saving orphans from a towering inferno, the ghosts always followed us and attacked at the most inopportune moment.

One springtime morning at recess, we were crouched behind the red brick wall of the school, hiding from a giant robot that wanted to turn us into robots that would turn people into robots. So far, we had evaded its clever tactics, although Jenny's foot had gotten stuck in some quicksand, and the robot had touched her foot, and so now she had a robot foot.

"I think we should make a run for swings," I said. "The robot is looking the other way."

"Let's do it," said Chad.

"Good idea," said Jenny. "My robot foot makes it so I can run extra fast."

"I don't think we should," said Benji.

"Why, not?" I asked.

"Because," said Benji, "the ghosts are over by the swing set!"

We all looked at the same time and, sure enough, the red, pink, orange, and cyan colors of our archenemies hovered near our only escape route, waiting for our next move.

"The ghosts!" exclaimed Jenny.

"That's our only way out," said Chad.

He was right. There was no other escape. We were doomed.

A frustration and anger built up inside me as I realized we had fallen into another trap. How could the ghosts outsmart us every time!? They must have had this planned all along. It wasn't fair. *We* were the heroes after all, and we had already defeated the ghosts countless times before. Yet somehow, they kept returning and hatching evil schemes to ruin our fun. It didn't make sense. I would not stand for it. Not this time. Someone had to do something to stop these evildoers.

I felt a surge of energy well up in my chest as my mouth opened and said, "Guys, come on! The ghosts can't always be there every time."

I didn't know then how easy it was to defeat a superhero and destroy a dream. I didn't know how fragile our powers were and how they could vanish as quickly as they had appeared. And I didn't know that stepping outside of yourself was all that it took.

The other members of my team looked at me as my words hung in the air, distorting the schoolyard the way that gas fumes bend light in the desert. A quick glance at the swing set revealed that the ghosts had vanished and the robot was no longer tearing up the teacher's parking lot. For a brief moment, I thought we were victorious and I had saved us from our most dreadful enemy.

But then I saw it: Benji's energy sphere no longer shimmered in psychedelic patterns around us. The ancient talisman that I used to cast my energy nets was transformed into a cheap plastic ring from a supermarket vending machine. Jenny's robot foot was just a regular foot and Chad could no longer fire lasers from any of his fingers.

Our powers were gone. And it was my fault.

In my defense, it was a fair point. It was ridiculous to think the ghosts would just *happen* to be there every time we were on an adventure. I mean, it's one thing to have an archnemesis ... But every goddamned time we were doing anything, a member of our team would suddenly see the ghosts and we'd be forced to contend with their attack. It was just lazy storytelling.

As the realization set in, we recognized how unrealistic the rest of our exploits had been. Our laser beams became *ideas* of laser beams, and our secret base suddenly looked a lot like the garage. Doors that used to lead to hidden passageways now led to my dad's office. Flying motorcycles transformed into stationary exercise bikes. Buttons that used to fire photon torpedoes now merely activated the rear defroster. Everything became heartbreakingly normal and mundane.

So, with all due respect, I think I'd like to resign from this superhero league before that sort of thing happens again. You see, I like believing in us and what we're doing here. I like how much we matter. I like how the low-budget plays we mount in small black box theaters stop wildfires and slay dragons. I like how our open-mic nights fend off interstellar death rays and our burlesque hula hoop routines liberate oppressed nations.

But I'm scared. My Spidey sense is tingling and I can feel the fiendish nemesis of self-awareness just beyond the horizon, waiting to strike. I mean, I don't have Spidey sense. That's Spider-Man's thing and, frankly, I think it's a little non-specific and as far as I know, it is not even a trait that spiders actually have, which makes you wonder where he even ... Oh, God. It's happening already.

I'm starting to worry about how much of my life would vanish if I stopped believing in it, just like those ghosts by the swing set. Because nothing was more important to me than those adventures, and nothing seems more ridiculous when I think about them now. And every superpower I've had since has fallen victim to the same fate: The love that I shared with a partner, the new play that was going to change the world, the paper-maché puppet that would thaw the heart of a hedge-fund broker.

Which is why I've developed this strategy of leaving early. Because it doesn't matter if our superpowers make us bulletproof or able to withstand a nuclear blast. They are as delicate as whimsy and our deepest convictions are merely passing through our heads on their way to someplace more interesting.

Citizens of Earth and Fellow Supers, please don't take my resignation personally. I really believe in what you're doing here. I am so inspired by the fearless feats of derring-do, love, and creative genius I see every day. But I have sworn an oath to protect your world. And I fear that if I do not leave it now, then I will be its downfall.

I bid you farewell.

Yours in everlasting heroism,
The Cynic

NERD: THE NEXT GENERATION

NICOLE GREEVY

"I want it!" my son shrieks.

We're in Target. My three-year-old son Griffin loves Target. He especially loves the dollar aisle. It's not the toy section, but he's figured out he stands a better chance of Mama or Daddy getting him something from the dollar aisle than he does the toy section. Preschoolers, like politicians, are experts in the art of the possible. We are in the dollar aisle. And I know what he's looking at.

It's a felt tiara, yellow, with a red star. Griffin spotted it on a previous trip, along with felt masks for Batman, Green Lantern, and the Flash. Last week, Griffin's daddy bought him the masks, but not the tiara. Clearly, Griffin hasn't forgotten about it.

Wonder Woman. My son loves her.

I have no idea when his allegiance shifted from the World's Greatest Detective and the Last Son of Krypton to the Amazonian Princess. Honestly, I wasn't even aware of Wonder Woman registering on him. It might have been *The Challenge of the Superfriends*, or *Justice League*; I have no idea. But right now, she's on top of his superhero rankings. And it makes me anxious.

I'm afraid he'll be picked on. I'm afraid he is a nerd. Like his mom.

My life feels like one long attempt to fit in. But I've never been able to. I've never been able to be interested in what "regular" people liked. Especially growing up. It drove my mother nuts. I had a temper tantrum when she painted my room pink. On the rare occasion she would let me buy something frivolous at the store, I picked a comic book (which I was only permitted to read in the privacy of my stupid pink room).

I still remember the issue, *Legion of Superheroes*, #265. The story was a mash-up of *Brigadoon* and *Roots*. Two years later, my brother was given the box set of *Dungeon & Dragons, Basic Edition*, but I'm the one who became a Dungeon Master. And in the wake of my mother's death, I discovered *Doctor Who* on PBS, *Buck Rogers in the 25th Century* in syndication, and that most kids had nothing but derision for a chubby girl who liked fantasy, sci-fi, and superheroes.

Being a nerd sucks (and yes, I'm aware that nowadays people like to distinguish between "nerd" and "geek" and what I am is technically a geek. To which I reply, "Shut up, dork. In my day they were the same thing."). I had no interest in the things more socially acceptable kids were into and, even worse, I couldn't keep my mouth shut about what I liked. When my local PBS station stopped airing *Doctor Who*, I couldn't grieve in private. No, I made a petition demanding it be aired again, and brought the petition to school to try to get the other kids to sign. When assigned to write an anonymous essay about a secret desire, I wrote about how I wished I was my favorite D&D character. So much for a hidden identity. And everyone knew I was rushing home from school to catch reruns of *Scooby Doo, Where Are You?* (I watched without irony.)

For ten years, my best friend was my shield against the ridicule. She liked many of the same things I did: Greek mythology, Breyer horses, and *Doctor Who*. As long as I had her on my side, I wasn't aware of other kids' opinions of me. But she was always "more" than me—smarter, more creative, more observant, and she was aware. Our friendship ended in 9th grade. It's hard to be a nerd, but it's also hard to be a nerd's friend. Immediately, effortlessly, she slipped in with a cooler crowd, who listened to Echo and the Bunnymen and The Jesus & Mary Chain and made fun of people who liked toy horses and *Doctor Who*, and I realized at some point in our friendship she'd stopped sharing my interests and started humoring them. Maybe it was in middle school when she strongly advised me against pasting pictures of Peter Davison as the 5th Doctor on my math folder. Whenever it was, I didn't see it because I hadn't wanted to. I couldn't bear to. But finally she'd had enough and moved on. And without her as my shield, for the first time, I got a very clear view of the other kids.

I saw how they looked at me. I heard every mean thing they whispered. I was lonely. I hated who I was. And the thought that my son might end up feeling about himself the way I felt about myself makes me sick to my stomach.

But I can't tell Griffin that. He's three years old and runs up to kids he doesn't know to ask, "Will you play with me?" He doesn't judge himself the way I judged myself—the way, sometimes, I still judge myself. And so I buy him the damn Wonder Woman tiara, and we go home. And I put the 1977 *Wonder Woman* series on the computer for him and he settles in to watch the Amazon Princess fight the Nazis.

And Todd's key turns in the lock, and he comes home. And Griffin looks up from the screen, felt tiara slightly askew, and says, "I'm Wonder Woman!"

"That's great, Griffy," Todd says, and disappears into the bedroom. I follow.

Todd stands turned away from me. Todd did better in high school than I did. He wasn't part of the popular crowd, but he was just on the outskirts. He knew how to fit in. He did fit in. He didn't buy Griffin a Wonder Woman tiara. And I know he's upset, not "angry upset," but worried upset. Like I am.

I put my hand on his shoulder and say, "He saw it at Target and I didn't know what to do. I mean, I don't know if he's even thinking of her as a, you know, woman. I think to him she's just a superhero so she's cool."

I hate that I'm even saying this. I hate that I am trying to rationalize my son pretending to be a female superhero, not because I have any opinion about his gender identity (he'll be who he'll be), but I'm afraid he'll be picked on for it. I don't want him to be a nerd. I don't want him to be like me.

"No, I get it. It's what he wanted," Todd says. "I just need to … wrap my head around it. I mean, yeah, I feel weird about it, but that's about me, not him. It's okay. I'm glad you got it for him."

There's a picture of a six-year-old Todd in our bedroom. He's wearing a hunting coat, holding a rifle, with a spaniel dog at his side.

Todd grew up in Oklahoma, and this is exactly how I might have pictured a regular, average kid from Oklahoma.

Except the picture is totally staged. The story behind the picture, as Todd told me, is that he had found one of his mom's dresses and put it on. He remembers he loved watching the fabric flutter as he moved—it just looked so cool. And he started pretending he was someone else. He was pretending to be Rita Moreno.

When his dad found out, he freaked, took the dress off, slapped a hunting coat over Todd's pajamas, pushed a gun in his hand and took a photo. A talisman. A shield.

I love this story. Because the photo didn't change anything. Todd had no interest in hunting, or sports, or any of the things regular Oklahoma kids liked. He liked superheroes and monster movies and sang in show choir and performed in dozens of musicals. And hey, a six-year-old who idolized Rita Moreno? That's some first-rate nerding right there.

I rejoin Griffin in the living room where he is getting bored with Linda Carter as Diana Prince in her military suit and owl spectacles. "Where's Wonder Woman?" he asks.

"That is Wonder Woman," I say. "She's in her secret identity right now. You know, like when Clark Kent transforms into Superman in that movie we watched."

"Well, when is she going to open her shirt?"

"Son," Todd calls from the bedroom, "I have been asking that since the 1970s."

Todd's saying that to make me laugh. And I do laugh. Because 20 years after high school, I'm not alone. I'm married to a man I adore, who actually bragged to his friends about our first Christmas when I gave him the special edition of *Halloween* with a collectible Michael Myers snow globe. And today superhero movies are the summer blockbusters, and HBO's biggest show features lots of dungeons <u>and</u> dragons, and 100 million people worldwide watched the 50th Anniversary special of *Doctor Who*.

I wasn't wrong about the things I loved; I was just a couple decades ahead of my time. Maybe the real reason people pick on nerds is deep down, they have a little bit of envy because we're trailblazers. *All your pop culture are belong to us.*

Anyway, my son is not a nerd yet. Right now, he's just Son of Nerd, and I need to let him be who he is. So he can fulfill his own destiny. Besides, grade school is still a long way away and I have a pretty great three-year-old right now, demanding I take a photo of him, wearing his tiara, waving his magic lasso.

I take his picture. It's fine. He's fine. I'm fine. I did, after all, survive high school. In fact, I even went to prom. Junior year I started going to *The Rocky Horror Picture Show* and was soon hanging out with kids from other high schools who also enjoyed spending their weekend nights shouting rude things at a movie screen. So, while the school week was still lonely, the weekends were great, filled with fishnets and rice and toast and parties and friends, friends, friends. One of these friends and I went to prom together. I bought a *Vogue* pattern and sewed my dress because it was an unimaginable *faux pas* to show up in the same outfit as anyone else. But when I think about it now, I know we were really all dressed alike. The girls wore dresses, tight on top, flowy on bottom, in a heavy fabric that shimmered. The boys all wore suits in virtually identical shapes, in dark colors that all blended into the same shade on the dance floor. No one wanted to stand out, get pointed at, or look ridiculous. And no one did. I'm sure we all thought we were dressing to be unique, to show off who we were, or wished we were, but in fact, we were all perfectly appropriate. Perfectly anonymous.

But today's nerds, the girl gamers and the bronies and the cosplayers and the LARPers, while they're being picked on, teased, tormented, they're pushing the envelope. They are challenging quietly, passively, anxiously, how we see what's normal and not, what's expected and not. And they're going to take us some pretty cool places. My son's prom is in 15 years. Maybe the pictures at his prom will show him and his date, hell, everyone at prom, costumed in a hundred different brilliant colors, in fabrics that flutter when they move, that shape their bodies into dozens of different silhouettes, that stretch and sparkle and shine in the light. And they

87

won't look ridiculous. They'll look amazing. Like gemstones. Like butterflies.

Like superheroes.

ALUMNI SHOW

July 17th, 2014
The Astoria Bookshop | Queens

Podcast Episode 5

"Snake Dreams"
written by Marcos Stafne
and performed by Jeff Wills

"Errant"
written by Jeff Wills
and performed by Marcos Stafne

No, YOU Tell It! participants are called "alumni." One doesn't need a degree to qualify as an alum. We can use the word for former members of any group. Still, completing the cycle of an *NYTI* show feels like a certain graduation. We come out of this unique process changed, with improved skills, personal insights, and broadened perspectives.

Marcos Stafne and I had been colleagues for two years before we met in his apartment for the start of this first alumni *NYTI*. Nevertheless, I was intimidated by him. I started working as an assistant at the art museum where he was Director of Education in 2012. So by "colleagues," I essentially mean a few hallway waves and memos with our names on them. I remember bringing a bottle of wine to his apartment for the writing session, because … uh, don't you do that? For visits? To directors…?

It turned out we have a lot in common, including a background in theatre. Workshopping our stories that summer, we both produced quite personal "personal narratives," which meant we discussed raw feelings about ourselves, our own lives. That's the sort of thing therapists often have to pry out of us, and I'd never been in another writing group with such assured "oh my God" moments.

That's what it is to witness someone craft their story, to learn about their failings and courage, about them as a whole person. The gratifying sucker-punch of *NYTI* is that, even in the midst of that revealing stage of the process, the real vulnerability is yet to come.

As we geared up for the show, we writer/performers parted to work with directors on performing our partner's completed story. Marcos and I were both reminded, I'm sure, of our days on stage. There's a new drive that takes over, one to honor the words you watched your story-partner work so hard on. I was fortunate in this regard, given Marcos' hilarious writing about the absurd number of times he was forced to confront a great fear. I think he had the harder job delivering my analogy between a lost, questing knight and a morning commute, all written from the second-person perspective.

You are so tied up in crafting your performance, in living up to your friend's hard-won words, that the last stage of this process sneaks up on you. You arrive at The Astoria Bookshop, taking critical mental notes with the deft eye of a seasoned performer. The seating arrangement, the traffic patterns of the small shop still operating while you'll perform, the occasional rumble of the nearby elevated train. Now fully prepared, you sit in your folding chair beside the storyteller's podium.

"Oh my God."

Somehow, even this second time participating in *NYTI*, I wasn't prepared for the simple act of sitting, and listening. There is a profound sense of receptivity in sitting in front of a group and doing nothing but listening to someone else live your story. It's a special feeling of vulnerability, transporting you to an immediate, new perspective on yourself.

When a show is complete, no one hands an alum of *NYTI* a diploma, shakes their hand, or claps their shoulder. The impulse is more to share a hug. You've gotten through something unique and profound and are better for it. I got to walk in a museum director's shoes through his whole, very human career, a huge opportunity for someone like me starting out.

Marcos let me know later on that my story gave him an appreciation for the ever-present struggles of parenting in New York City. Listening, I learned it was okay—healing, even—to laugh at my struggles, while somehow also feeling supported in them by a room full of people.

I'm grateful for the process that produced what you'll read here. If I could frame that experience and hang it on my wall, I surely would.

SNAKE DREAMS

MARCOS STAFNE

The first time I met Fantasia, she was eating a guinea pig in front of several children. Watching this grotesque act was a "required rite of passage" at the museum—a program called *Fantasia's Feeding Frenzy*. I had heard about the large, albino Burmese python that lived at the end of a tunnel at the museum, but didn't quite understand everyone's warnings of how big she really was. This snake could easily eat a baby or a toddler. Or kill me. That was what my mind jumped to when I saw her swallowing the guinea pig ... her fourth during that *Frenzy*. Fantasia could kill me, and she was now my responsibility as the new director of all things large and small at the children's museum in Brooklyn. She was just one of the larger things, and by "large" we were talking 20 feet long and 300 pounds.

When I dream, I have nightmares about snakes. When snakes dream, do they fantasize about torturing me?

Growing up in Florida, you're taught two skills to survive our natural wildlife: (1.) If an alligator is chasing you, run in a zigzag pattern, and (2.) stay away from all snakes. If you think you can tell a venomous snake from a friendly snake with some sort of rhyme or memory nugget from a 4th grade science class, you will be bit before you remember if "red touching black is a friend of Jack." Florida has six venomous snakes, and they're everywhere. On top of that, we have dangerous, stupid people who collect even more dangerous snakes, breed them, then get drunk or high on meth and let them out of their Tupperware containers. This means that on occasion there is a random cobra or mamba roaming around a golf course and Burmese pythons (snakes so big, they can swallow alligators) swimming around the Everglades.

My fear of snakes comes from both nature and nurture. I believe I am genetically inclined to fear snakes. When I see a snake, or something that slightly looks like a snake, my entire body painfully recoils in terror. My chest muscles contract, forcing the breath out of my body, and my eyes shut tight. This is slightly embarrassing, especially around winter when I catch someone folding a scarf out of the corner of my eye. There is no rational reason for a large snake to be crawling around a table of scarves, but I can't control the reaction my body has trying to protect me from scarf bites.

Before all 20 feet of Fantasia slithered into my life, I had been involved with corn snakes 1 and 2. They were part of the world's scariest work orientation at a science center in Florida—a much-desired job with no indication of the required snake wrangling on the application. I had been hired to be a program presenter, a great part-time job for a theatre major interested in science. My first assignment at the center was to prepare for a program called *Reptiles and Amphibians*. In my mind I thought it would be a fun show-and-tell with turtles and frogs. No one had mentioned snakes—that program would have obviously been called *Reptiles and Devil Sticks*. Not wanting to lose my new job, I sheepishly told a friendly coworker I didn't like snakes. I tried to play it off as an, "oh, you know, I've just never been around one, and I wouldn't want to hurt it" kind of situation. She said I would be fine and she would train me to be a snake wrangler in three easy steps.

The first step was being in a small room with a snake. A day later, I was to touch the snake, gently, with two fingers. On my third day I was supposed to hold the snake. This apparently qualified me to stand in front of an audience and pretend to be an expert about reptiles. None of this plan went well.

When I stood in the room with corn snakes 1 and 2, I could feel their non-blinking eyes focus on my delicious fingers ... ready to strike. Chest clenched. No breath. Eyes shut. I left the room defeated. I had a nightmare that night in which snakes lived in my pillows. The next day when I had to touch red corn snake 1—gently, with two fingers—I almost passed out. My kind coworker saw my slow introduction to snake wrangling was not working out, so she explained a psychological trick that might help me. I was to imagine a dollar amount in my head every time I had to pick up the snake.

At the time I made $5.25 an hour, so as I put my hand into the devil cage, I thought: "$5.25 ... $5.25 ... Fuck, I'm touching a snake ... $5.25 ... Please don't bite me ... $5.25 ... $5.25 ... This is the worst thing I have ever done ... $5.25." The $5.25 trick worked enough in that, while I spat out a very scripted discussion of snakes and their virtues to 5th graders crammed into an auditorium, I was somehow able to split my mind from my body to get through each program. But I could never look at the snake directly. I was always amazed that the kids who watched my *Reptile and Devil Sticks* show did not freak the fuck out like I did each and every single time.

They did, however, ask a lot of questions. Questions that I always had to answer in half-truth statements: "Do snakes feel slimy?"

Half-truth statement: "Well, no, they feel cool and smooth, and their scales are quite dry." I wanted to say that they feel like cold, dead sticks that wrap around your arms—dead sticks that can bite you or coil their cold bodies around your throat until you die.

"Do snakes bite?"

"Well anything with a mouth bites, but our snakes are handled on a daily basis and are quite tame."

The reality: Snakes do whatever the fuck they please. Some snakes are mean and bite you for the hell of it. Some snakes, the ones you would never imagine biting you—the half-dead ones who have been used by nature centers for their entire lives—will just surprise-bite you in the middle of a program at exactly the moment when you are telling an audience how tame a snake can be.

"What do snakes eat?"

"Well, we feed snakes small mice, but in the wild they eat what they can find."

The reality: Every snake we had in a mixed enclosure—a fancy aquarium with more than two species of animal inside of it—tried to eat anything smaller than the snake. I once walked into work to find a snake that died trying to eat another snake. I've even seen a snake try to eat its own tail, which is slightly sad, because it means the snake has neurological damage—and no one wants that for any living creature.

I worked with snakes on-and-off for about five years and it never got easier to hold one, but I learned to tolerate it. Fast-forward 17 years and many museum jobs later, many jobs in snake-free environments, and I was now confronted with my dream administrative museum job, except for the snake parts. Approaching daily life with Fantasia was going to be a challenge. I had been in the presence of a few giant snakes during random museum festivals and events, but they were mostly handled by macho-snake-dudes—guys who really dug giant constrictors and showed them off in casual, nonchalant ways that projected, "oh this 20-foot, 300-pound thing ... it's no big deal."

This casual snake handling unnerved me to no end. It was how I first encountered Fantasia. She struck at her guinea pig with extreme force while her "macho-snake-dude" stood by the open door to her enclosure.

"Can't she get out?" I asked. The coworker who had dragged me down to see the *Feeding Frenzy* answered that she didn't move much, except when she was hungry. I noticed a small container of clear liquid by her enclosure, next to a bucket of thawed-out guinea pigs. "What's that liquid?" I asked, thinking it was some sort of medicine. "Oh, that's vodka. You use that to throw in her mouth in case she bites you. I think it helps to release her jaws."

I later learned that snakes that size require two people to be with them at all times during feedings. You know, just in case ... but nothing's happened in ... you know ... a while ... Oh, and the magic vodka will fix everything.

Fantasia had been a pet rescue in the early 2000s. She had actually been much smaller, and probably outgrew her New York City apartment. This happens to a lot of pets in NYC including Rottweilers, iguanas, and other really large pythons. People obtain these animals illegally, and when they can't take care of them anymore, they just put them out on the street. In Florida, people just release these animals into the wild and they seem to make it. In New York, if you let a snake out, it usually dies in the cold.

The act of rescuing Fantasia was filled with great intentions, and she quickly became a favorite of visitors and a teaching tool on the perils of improper pets. She also became too big ... too quickly. She outgrew her enclosure and had to have a bigger one built for her. She also liked to eat a lot, and she got testy if she was hungry. The process of slimming down a snake can be long and dangerous work.

There's not a lot of information about maintaining a Burmese python in captivity. We found out that the oldest pythons can live to be up to 27 years old. When I met Fantasia, she was just turning 19, so there was a possibility of her staying alive for 8 more years. Interesting factoid about snakes: They never stop growing, and with the possibility of another 7 or 8 years left in her, we had to think about an even bigger enclosure.

The museum had invested a lot of marketing material into Fantasia, and she had become a mascot and staff favorite. I was puzzled about how people spoke about her as if she had some sort of non-snake, Mrs. Doubtfire personality. People said she was friendly, kind, and loved to teach children. I never saw any of that. What I saw, one time, was Fantasia yawning. Imagine a snake yawning—it's a lot like a snake about to bite you in slow motion. This sight caused me to have horrible nightmares where Fantasia attacked me, or just popped up in the backseat of my car.

We held two events annually when we took her out for visitors to meet her. I was coerced into letting this happen, as it had become a sick tradition. What could ever happen when you let a 300-pound python out to visit with rabbit-sized kids? I did muster the willpower to be present with her in the room. After spending an hour or so with her two maintainers, and the emergency vodka, I gathered just enough courage to touch her. The keeper guided her head into my hand.

For a moment I forgot she was a snake. I imagined being in the presence of a dinosaur—some sort of long-necked baby diplodocus. She pressed my hand down, and I could sense how powerful she was—just pure muscle choosing not to strike because she was mildly bored. After about an hour she chose to go back into her enclosure where it was warm, and we didn't stop her. We couldn't really stop her from doing much—including leaving when she wanted to—which was what she did one warm August day.

I sat in our president's office chatting before a much-needed vacation to Norway. As in: I was about to get on a plane to Norway in three hours. Norway, a country with cute trolls and no visible snakes in the marketing material. One of my staff members ran into the office and said, "Fantasia just got out and she bit someone. You should probably come down NOW."

Chest clutched. No breath. Eyes shut. You're in charge now, Marcos. Go figure this out.

The president and I walked briskly down the long tunnel through a crowd of very stunned visitors. We found her writhing in a corner on the ground, tangled in a number of red stanchions used to keep visitors away from the *Feeding Frenzy*. Apparently, Fantasia had missed her guinea pig while striking and accidently latched on to her keeper's leg. The other "required person" had to enact the emergency vodka plan, which seemed to just make Fantasia dazed and confused. She did, however, finally detach from her keeper.

With the calm of St. Patrick, I asked all non-essential personnel to leave the room. Fantasia's main keeper was taken to the hospital, and I was left with the giant snake in the corner. One of our more adventurous staff members tried to coerce her back into her enclosure by standing in her giant cage, dangling a guinea pig in front of her, and saying, "Here snakey snakey, here snakey snakey." This was not the wisest of choices, so I had to step in.

I shouted at him, "Get out of her cage now!" The president stood next to me and calmly urged me not to shout. I redirected my fear to say, "Hey, that snake is dazed and agitated. I am not prepared to wrestle her off of you today. I will not die for you today." This is something I had to say at work … about the giant 300-pound snake in the room. He stepped down from the enclosure and stepped behind me. Time seemed to freeze. Blurs of people came in and out of the room with me mostly telling them to leave — there was no need to stare at the situation, especially when the situation could slither over and start some trouble. The fire department came, walked into the room, and I told them to walk back out, which they did, happily.

Fantasia was not on fire, and there was nothing they could do. She would eventually get cold and want to go back into her enclosure.

I watched Fantasia meander for about an hour until we got some help to wrangle her back into the enclosure—one of those macho-snake-dudes I was usually annoyed with came to my rescue. Fantasia was completely fine. I left after her keeper came back from the hospital. She was fine, too.

Half-truth: This type of thing happens at similar institutions all the time, and we made all the right decisions.

The reality: That was some scary shit. My super-calm president handled all of the collateral questions that came up when a big snake nipped her keeper. I somehow found myself on a train to the airport. I was safe inside the LIRR, and when I finally sat down, I realized my entire body had been clenched with fear for three hours. The process of releasing giant snake tension was not easy. I made it to my plane to Norway with only a mild nervous breakdown in the international terminal of JFK.

I knew in my heart that this was the last straw, and we would need to find a different home for Fantasia, and we did. She was moved to the Staten Island Zoo, and just after her 20th birthday, Fantasia died of natural causes.

One of our trustees said she probably died of a broken heart.

My heart was not broken. A week ago I dreamt that Fantasia attacked me in a classroom at the museum. I used to have dreams about regular snakes attacking me; now I have dreams about giant snakes attacking me. I'm empathetic that people have sad feelings about Fantasia's death, but empathy is not sympathy, and I refuse to feel sad about her leaving.

There's a new pine snake at the museum named Roger. For some reason, I really like Roger, and I think it's solely because of his name. He came to the museum at the same time as Jeremy, the bearded dragon. Roger and Jeremy are small reptiles that can teach kids about animals, and when I think about them, I pretend they are members of our IT department—they are my coworkers, after all. They don't inspire the awe and wonder of Fantasia, but sometimes that much

101

awe and wonder aren't what's best for urban kids who have never seen a reptile. Roger and Jeremy don't require an emergency vodka plan.

ERRANT

JEFF WILLS

Then he smote the steed with his spurs, and sprang on his way, so that sparks flew from the stones after him ... [he] went his way swiftly, and rode many a wild road ... So many wonders did that knight behold, that it were too long to tell the tenth part of them. ... Yet he cared not so much for the strife; what he deemed worse was when the cold clear water was shed from the clouds, and froze ere it fell on the fallow ground. —Sir Gawain & the Green Knight

You get out the front door and watch the 7:24 Q18 bus stopped at the light, almost literally at your doorstep. But the sidewalk is an ice sheet, and your wife has your baby strapped to her, and her winter boots are in for repair, so she's wearing galoshes, so you have to take it slow, so you can't make it the half-block to your right to the bus stop before the bus has already moved there, picked up passengers — and even waited for a woman running after it — before pulling away with a roar. But there's another bus that's due in ten minutes.

It gets there in twenty. The driver makes a teenager get up from the reserved-for-disabled seat so your wife and child can rest. But it's crowded, and standing near them means you're blocking the aisle, so you move along to a precarious stance at the back doorway. For nearly a mile, you're apart.

In the interim, you think. You think about needs. You need to move, to shorten this daily journey. You need more money just to pay the daycare, much less incur moving expenses. You need time with your daughter, more than an hour a day between here and there. You need to talk. With your wife. The days are a continuum of rigorous schedule, necessary and tightly packed order, capped off with maybe an exhausted hour just at the end if you last that long. You are snipping and snapping your way through them, your humor ravaged by the horde of needs. But enough of that now.

You rush to push through that back door and run along the bus's side over a rock-hard ridge of former snow to reach the front door, to help your wife and child down the rubbery bus stairs and over the self-same ice mound. Then it's up the steel, diamond-studded stairs to the outdoor elevated subway stop where the wait is not too bad, and the train is not too crowded. No one offers your wife a seat.

At the next transfer, the platform is thick with people ready to board the train you're exiting. A young man plows in as soon as the doors open, in defiance of the masses exiting. Your wife, with a grim swiftness, evades him, only just keeping her balance as she twists the 25 pounds of toddler out of his ignorant, arrogant, barreling way.

New, urgent needs lance their way into the yawning space of the quarter-second between his invasion and your escape. A need to teach a lesson, a need to see him fall, a need to feel the percussion of his ribcage through the bottom of your boot. You could yell, but he wouldn't hear, and it would add to your wife's considerable stress, and there isn't time.

But you also don't need to get out of his way, and you don't. And maybe, just maybe, you get a little more in it.

You regroup, bracing for the next stage of this pilgrim's progress. This platform is better sheltered, and you don't have too long to wait for the train. This car is packed, so you just manage to press in after your swift wife and dazed daughter. A young man pushes upward through the mass to offer your wife his seat, which she accepts with a weary smirk. You marvel once again at how chivalry can rally.

When the door at your back opens at the first underground station, you have to step outside momentarily to allow people room to disembark. As soon as you do, hand still clutched to the mechanical door (as though you had the strength to stop it closing) you hear your daughter wail in shock at your seeming abandonment. You can just make out your wife's soothing whispers in patient prayer under the cry. You edge back on, and because you can't reach her, you just do your best with a smile you don't feel and,

"I'm right here. I'm right here."

Her face doesn't quite relax, her faith restored only for the moment.

You're at the stop and disembark, taking advantage of a narrow space between twin iron ceiling supports to thin out the approaching riot of commuters rushing to board. You act as a guide and shield to get the lot of you past the lottery of turnstiles pouring forth sprinting adults. Inevitably, somewhere in the progress between the platform and the busy five-way intersection at the top of the stairs, someone or two or three has gotten between you and your family.

For seconds, you're reminded of what it was like to be what once you were. Young. Barging onto a train for your own urgent reasons. Offering up your seat and feeling a glow for a few minutes after. Springing up steps two-at-a-time on spry legs and, once above, heading in whatever direction suited you. Young. Needing nothing.

There they are at the corner, and from her mount on your wife's torso, your daughter is looking for you, and that's really all there is or needs to be. You replace her hat and/or mittens as necessary (your child's, not your wife's) and slowly navigate the gestalt of them over slush lakes and more leaden moguls to start the half-mile trek to the shore.

The sidewalk is narrowed by frozen precipitate and vehicles straddling the curb, and in various places completely blocked by edifices of scaffolding. You hold your wife's hand again, making slow progress and frequently walking ahead to allow others to pass in both directions. Her chin dimples as she edges her jaw forward. Your brow sprouts crevices of concentration. You haven't spoken in nearly half an hour.

You need to ignore your instincts. If you feel her slip or clutch, you must hang on, pull up, or engulf. That much is easy. But if *your* traction gives, if *your* purchase on the path is in peril, you must—above all else—LET GO. You try not to think of the consequences if you fall, and fail, so you practice it in your mind as you ford another confounding intersection, which bears not one stop sign, in spite of a riotous current of traffic coming from all four points of the compass.

Finally, you arrive at daycare. There is still a suction-sealed front door, and soaked linoleum hallways under your wife's galoshes, and undoing, removing, replacing, and redoing your endless boots to enter-then-exit the room. But no one has fallen. And—truly miraculous—the little one is thrilled to be there.

Warmth. Relief. Your daughter is delivered unto the loving arms of paid strangers. A kiss goodbye, adorable, and maybe an extra blown kiss if she's facing the right way, and not too distracted by her waffles and banana and toddling friends.

You are the victor. A winter soldier, come in from the cold. As a reward, you have only now to get your wife to work without cracking her head against the hard, frozen city.

The cold again, and the quarter-mile walk, and the feeling every single time that you've forgotten something because you're carrying two fewer bags and one fewer human being. You hold hands with your wife, except when you can't, and brave the stopless intersection and sub-arctic, sub-aquatic, five-point intersection, and head back down into the final stop before Manhattan.

And you wait. And you wait.

A train comes, but it's too congested with passengers to board, and anyway the subway is a hydra, and two more would spring forth in its place. You're behind already; five minutes will not suffer more.

The next train that comes is similarly devoid of air, especially after dozens more people cut you off to cram in. So you wait.

As does the train. It sits there with its doors open, stoic. A snoring beast, unconcerned with your nearness. On the fifth cycle of its motors warming up, then cooling down, there's still no announcement. Now the platform's population density mirrors the train's interior. A transit officer strides down the unspoken aisle from wherever he mysteriously apparated. Now you know it's serious.

There is nothing to see. No hint evident. There is no announcement. But there is a human being, and he is walking with a purpose. It's most likely someone "sick." "Sick" can mean so many things here in the underworld. And now you're no longer behind, but truly late.

So. You tell your wife you'll walk to the nearest alternate route, and she resets her jaw and comes with you. You trundle through the human aisle, against the current, back through the stiles and back up the steps. A woman ahead of you heralds for all descending that there's a "sick passenger," and you wonder at why you never perform this public service, and simultaneously how she can be so sure with no official proclamation. Her quest, not yours.

You and your wife make the walk, which is not quite a mile, fortunately. Your fingertips ache, and you worry about her toes in her thin Rubbermaid footwear. The wind picks up. Every inch of the winding trail is some permutation of frozen, and you feel a pulling hunger for spring. You're never quite sure of the way to this station, but you know which directions are useful to turn (east - north - east - north - east...) until something looks familiar.

You descend once more. A train comes right away, also packed to the gills. But there's the promise of two different stripes that run through this station, so: You wait. And another train comes, without a molecule of oxygen. And you wait. And another train comes, gullet crammed. And you wait.

Suddenly there is one more train there, one of the newer ones, shining and comparatively spacious within, and by now you've moved to the middle of the platform in hopes of the guts of the train allowing more space. It pays off. Not only is there distinguishable room, but several people hastily disembark. You both step gratefully in, and feel a blast of warm air embrace you even as the doors close.

You smell the feces a moment later. The guts of the train, indeed.

You wonder—not for the first time—if it's something about adult human feces in general that triggers a primal need to run, flee, be safely away. Or if it is the fact that the adult human feces you're accustomed to inhaling is from the most desperate, malnourished, and long-neglected fellow adult humans. You look to the facing seats next to you there at the end of the car, and find not one, but an ignored occupant per each. Both wear pants that are dark, splotchy, and of a now-unknown material; one is balding in scarred patches of blight, or self-infliction.

But they're wearing pants, and visibly breathing, for which you feel some not-insignificant gratitude as you all tunnel together under the East River.

Your wife speaks. She asks if you want to switch cars at the next stop, shifting uncomfortably within her sleeping bag of a coat. But your transfer is the one just after that, and it's risky to switch cars, and if for some reason you can't get back on, you will lose what little reason is left to you. Perhaps you can get by with mouth breathing. So you say no, but leave her the option, which she decides to take. The train slows to the first stop in Manhattan, opening its side onto a tauntingly empty platform.

Your wife says, "Bye," then waits for her kiss. You hadn't expected this, thought because of your odorous companions and her overwhelming caution about germs that you'd have to forgo this ritual. You think; not of your needs, but of your wants. You share a kiss, and your heart beats the one-two of a thank-you.

She exits the car, hopping nimbly onto the next. Now you're alone. She is just past a couple of sets of sliding doors and a buffer of freezing damp wind, and you're amongst hundreds of fellow commuters, but you're alone.

The train pulls into its next stop—your transfer, and you do. Wondrously, it is not a walking transfer. So you simply step off, enjoying a very mild rush from once again breathing through your nose, and turn and lean back into the wall of the platform. The train doors close, sealing off its cargo. As it gallops past, you see your wife once more through the window of the following car, her head bowed and mouth moving in deference to her iPod's catechism of black-leather rock-n-roll.

Another train arrives shortly thereafter, and you board, and it's not too crowded. There are even seats. And after a few stops, when it seems clear the train ahead of it is picking up the majority of passengers and unlikely that someone will need it more than you, you allow yourself one of those seats.

You're on your way. You'll arrive soon. All hail the weary traveler.

NO REGRETS

August 14th, 2016
Fairleigh Dickinson University | New Jersey

Podcast Episode 67

"The First Tattoo"
written by Letisia Cruz
and performed by Heather Lang-Cassera

"In Spite of Ourselves"
written by Tazio Ruffilo
and performed by Letisia Cruz

"A Midwestern Purgatory"
written by Heather Lang-Cassera
and performed by Tazio Ruffilo

People often ask where I got the idea for *No, YOU Tell It!* I never know how to answer because instead of a single thunderbolt of thought, the idea came in a multitude of *plinks*, pooling together over time. I can say, however, that *No, YOU Tell It!* wouldn't exist without all I gained in Fairleigh Dickinson University's low-residency MFA in Creative Writing program.

Attending my first residency, I knew I had made the right choice. My fellow students hailed from all over the U.S., bringing with them diverse ages, occupations, and an amazing array of life experiences. I treasured those winter days we spent secluded together at FDU's campus in Wroxton, England, writing, laughing, and sharing stories at teatime. *Plink.*

That residency included the tradition of "New Student Night," where us newbies got up to read our writing. I remember huddling in the back of the pub with a young woman who was so scared, I thought she might have an embolism. Hands shaking, she whispered to me, "I wish I could read your story and you could read mine. Then this wouldn't be so terrifying." *Plink.*

I developed *No, YOU Tell It!* alongside earning my MFA in Creative Nonfiction. I was honored (and nervous!) when I was given the opportunity to bring the series to FDU's summer residencies in Madison, New Jersey after I graduated. Our first show, "Stargazing," was a hit! The following summer I chose the theme "No Regrets," since our show fell the morning after the graduation dinner—and big Saturday night dance party.

Ironic that as the residency approached, poet and artist Letisia Cruz emailed me with her regret over agreeing to participate. Terror had taken over, and she feared she would butcher reading someone else's story, confessing that "I have really horrible stage fright, and I can hardly get through a 30-second poem." *Plink.*

I replied, "Um, yeah, no, you aren't quitting," but way nicer. She didn't know it, but Leti's embolism-inducing panic—created by asking introverted writers to get up in front of an audience—was a huge part of why I started *No, YOU Tell It!* That night in the pub, holding that young writer's shaking hand, inspired us to make sharing personal stories less terrifying by trading tales. My background as an actress and playwright informed the idea further by supporting such storytellers through rehearsals with a theatrical director.

I assured Leti that this *show*, held Sunday morning while we all ate bagels, would be chill, and no one in the FDU community would judge her. I could say this with confidence because one of the core values of our series, "cooperation over competition," comes directly from what I love most about FDU's literary community. At the residencies, I never felt like we were competing to be the "best writer" but helping each other find the best way to tell our stories.

Most of all, I assured Leti I would be with her every step of the way. The residency allowed us plenty of time to rehearse her partner's story and, if she still didn't feel comfortable, I would step in and read for her. Embracing the less-scary idea of "chilling over bagels," Leti agreed to give it a go. As her friend, I didn't want Leti to regret quitting our "No Regrets" show. As a producer, I couldn't let her quit because, due to another storyteller already dropping out because of health issues, I'd created what is now the *NYTI* backup plan: The "tri-flip."

In a tri-flip, instead of partnering in pairs, the three participants trade tales around in a triangle. I'd admired the members of this FDU tri-flip, Letisia Cruz, Heather Lang-Cassera, and Tazio Ruffilo, for years before our performance and had a blast getting to know them in a whole new light that summer as their director.

Leti did not butcher Taz's story. In fact, a standout moment was when Leti gave one of his characters, a talking nail standing on its head in the road, a mocking accent:

114

I can do this forever, amigo.

Taz later shared, "I'll never think of that nail the same way."

When I think of that nail, I remember sitting there, eating my bagel, filled with pride and awe over how Leti went from barely being able to get through a poem to charming the entire audience with her quirky embodiment of an inanimate object.

More and more, we live in a world of immediacy, and I am grateful for the time and creative energy extended to me by the FDU and *NYTI* communities. The *plinks* of inspiration during my time at FDU contributed to the creation and evolution of *No, YOU Tell It!* and, in turn, the deep pool of storytellers willing to share in each other's stories gave me confidence in the value of my own.

Artwork by Letisia Cruz inspired by Tazio Ruffilo's story,
"In Spite of Ourselves"

THE FIRST TATTOO

LETISIA CRUZ

I rush to my locker and shove my books inside. I tell my friend Nina that I'll be back before the last bell. I rush down the hall, cut through the gym, and exit the back door. I walk to the bus stop on Belleville Avenue and take the 13 bus to Newark, then head to Penn Station and take the north train to Clifton. In roughly two hours, I will have a permanent black and blue butterfly on my chest. My heart beats fast as I walk toward the shop. I light a cigarette and focus on the exhale. It's 1990. I'm 14 years old.

I have known Nina since the seventh grade. She moved from Argentina the same year I left Union City and appeared in homeroom wearing a Doors t-shirt and combat boots. We become instant friends. On Friday nights we transcribe lyrics under a cloud of cigarette smoke in the basement as Jim Morrison's poetry fills the pages of our journals.

On my way back to school my skin buzzes. My chest is on fire and my limbs are shaky. On the train, I read a library book about butterflies and metamorphosis. I am convinced that the butterfly's spirit has entered my body through the needle of a tattoo gun. I have journeyed into a new state of being; I possess the ability to transform. Perhaps I am capable of flight. I arrive back at school and meet Nina at her locker. I flash a smile and my newly decorated chest. She runs an uncertain finger over my bloody skin and does not smile.

*

My father was once a political prisoner in Cuba; he later works nights at an electrical company in Paterson. On weekends, the five of us — my father, my mother, my grandfather, my sister and I — pack into the yellow Datsun and roam the streets looking for curbside furniture, or picnic under the George Washington Bridge if it is warm enough.

My father has a Minolta camera my mother gifted him for his last birthday. He uses it to take black and white pictures of my mother as she sits cross-legged on a park bench, stands over the kitchen sink of our Union City apartment, combs her hair near their bedroom window, and smiles only for him. From my father, I learn how to roller-skate, how to ride a bike, how to climb cliffs, how to understand bird calls, and how to yank my loose teeth out with a string.

When I am six years old, we visit a local pool hall. Old men drink beer and pretend to aim at cue balls while kids my age run in circles around the tables. I am not interested in running that day. Instead, I sit at the edge of the bar admiring the decorated arms of an ancient man. This is long before full sleeves are common, and I am mesmerized by the patterns. They seem as much a part of the man as his eyes or his nose. I am unable to formulate exactly how, but on some intuitive level I already know one day my arms will look like his.

Eventually, I will learn the word "tattoo." I will research ancient Nubian and Egyptian markings to find that the art dates back even further to the 4th millennium BC. I will come to believe some people are born with tattoos, and that life and experience eventually deliver these to the surface of our skin. I will fantasize about patterns emerging on my body and develop superstitions about what might trigger their manifestation.

My own culture, deeply steeped in folklore, will become the basis for my mythology. This will make sense, like the *azabaches* that all Cuban children wear to ward off the evil eye, or the glass of water under the bed used to guide the lost spirits of our ancestors toward the afterlife. I will keep a bucket on the fire escape that fills with rainwater when it storms and use it to bathe in an attempt to summon my markings. Of course, eventually I will come to understand that the only required ritual does not involve rainwater or invocation, but a simple tattoo gun and a needle.

Shortly after my ninth birthday, two bullets will end my father's life. I will not worry about his subsequent journey as much as I will obsess about his ability to connect with the past. I will light candles and burn drawings. I will consult the tarot, dream dictionaries, astrology charts, and the I-Ching. I will send smoke signals. I will carve directions on my skin.

Two weeks after my chest tattoo emerges, I sit on my bed lathering lotion. My room is a closet in the basement with no windows. I have chosen it because here I prefer the dark. It is early December and already my mother is anxious about Christmas. She stands in the hallway near the kitchen calling my name. It is Saturday morning and I've managed to avoid breakfast. I walk up the stairs in my white thermal top and sweatpants. I step into the hallway and instantly, she glares at my chest.

I become self-conscious and wrap my arms around myself. She points, and her face becomes distorted. Her eyes widen as if she's acquired x-ray vision. I run to the bathroom and she chases me, screaming something incoherent. I shove her hands back and shut the door. She pounds her fists on the other side and I worry the door's hollow core will give way—that her arms will come flailing through. But my mother goes quiet.

I examine myself in the mirror and discover that my mother has not acquired x-ray vision. A black blur *is* visible beneath my white thermal. It is almost obvious. I feel stupid for having been so careless. Had I been cautious, I could've covered my entire torso in butterflies without having to explain myself. Now that explanation seems inevitable.

The day my butterfly materializes, Nina and I walk to the abandoned reservoir after school. We sit on a rusted bench freezing our asses off and discussing symbolism. She tells me about the Argentine legend of Caráu, which tells the story of a young man whose mother is suffering from a deadly disease. The mother sends her son for medicine, but on his way to the village the boy hears an accordion and follows its sound. He forgets his purpose and begins dancing with a girl. Later, he learns that while he was dancing his mother has died.

The following morning he invites the young girl to accompany him back home, but she responds that his house is far away, and she will not journey with someone who does not care for his own mother. Heartbroken and alone, the young man is transformed into a Caráu bird, forever destined to bear black feathers and sing a mournful song.

I work part-time at an airbrush shop where I learn to draw Homie the Clown and Black Bart Simpson. I am paid weekly in cash, and I stuff every dollar into the hole of an owl I made in ceramics class. I fill my journal with sketches of disproportionate body shapes and use them to plot future tattoos: a bird on my back, vines on my ankle, a moon on my wrist. I become increasingly obsessed with mapping symbols and creating patterns—to what end? I can't say. Simply that the shapes are important. They mean something: *These words hurt; these vines have torn you apart; this moon will guide you; these flowers have the power to heal.*

I tip-toe out of the bathroom. My mother sits on the couch, her face buried in her hands. She sobs into her palms and the tears drift down her wrists and onto her chest. I don't know what to do, so I walk over to the sink and pour her a glass of water. I've seen my mother angry many times. I've seen her upset, too, and as a little girl I laid next to her countless nights as she cried herself to sleep. But never before this day have I ever felt her grief so interlaced with my own. I sit beside her and cry. Seeing me in tears, she asks if I regret getting the tattoo.

The truth is, I love the butterfly. I love feeling its scaly surface beneath my fingers. I love the way it buzzes on my skin, as if fluttering its wings. But most of all, I love its permanence—the way it is wholly mine, the way it can never leave me. So I say no. I do not regret the tattoo. But I don't want to be like Caráu. I fall silent because I can't find the words to express how every night the butterfly begs to take flight.

I sit under a large awning in the back terrace of my mother's house. It is early December in Miami and we're grilling burgers by the pool in 90-degree heat. The sky is grey and swollen; it feels as if any second the rain will break. I've just turned 36 and once again commemorated my birthday with a new tattoo. This one is a mermaid on my left thigh. My sister says she looks like a drawing from one of our children's books. I smile and tease that she is finally right about something.

"Whatever," she says, "I'm *always* right." My mother flips the last burger, lights a cigarette, and looks at my thigh. I like this one, she says. She looks happy.

We talk about the holidays and briefly mention goals for the New Year, but mostly discuss food preparations for *noche buena*. My sister points out that as usual my mother's menu will be enough to feed the entire neighborhood. "Remember that year mom found out about your first tattoo and hardly even cooked?" she says. "That was a shit Christmas." My mother half smiles and says I nearly gave her a heart attack.

My nephew walks out, pulls up a chair, and grabs a burger. "What are we talking about?" he asks.

"Just your tía's first tattoo," my sister says.

"Oh, cool. So which one was your first tattoo, tía?" my nephew asks.

I think about my first tattoo and realize they have never seen it. I tell my nephew that when I was his age, his mom and I drove 1,300 miles from New Jersey to Miami in a rusty van during a hurricane. "Of course, that was a long time ago," I say, "long before you came along, and long before this mermaid, or this moon, or any of these birds were here. I already had the butterfly. But the truth is that wasn't my first tattoo."

For a second there is silence, a collective observance of our past, and the recognition that we all found our own way to heal. Rain breaks and almost in unison, my mother bursts out laughing.

IN SPITE OF OURSELVES

TAZIO RUFFILO

I let a hitchhiker drive my car for a few hours while I slept in the back seat. When I met him standing out front of a beer, bait, ammo, lottery ticket, and cigarette shop in Georgia, holding a guitar case, he seemed like a nice enough guy. He told me he'd heard John Prine playing from my car when I pulled up. We talked about music for a minute, and he mentioned he's on his way to Houston. I told him I was headed in that direction. Before I pulled away he asked if I could drop him off somewhere in Texas. He didn't look intimidating and didn't smell bad, at least from where I stood. But, more than anything else, he caught me at the right time, fresh off a "get right" stop in the convenience store bathroom. I told him to hop in the car.

Now he's long gone with my bag that has enough drugs inside to get me to California. I wake up a few feet into a roadside field, under the stars, dripping sweat, and the skeeters are picking at me. I'm going through it again. Opiate withdrawal. I can't. I'd rather blow my fucking brains out. This cross-country trip was supposed to be my last hurrah before I got clean. I heard about this clinic out west that puts you in a medically induced coma while you're feeling your sickest. That's where I was headed.

"It'll be like time traveling," I said to myself when I first learned of the process. I'd fantasized about going to sleep and waking up a few years down the road, with a job using my degrees and living with the girl who left a long time ago. I'd have muscles everywhere, even on the back of my head, not a body looking like a wad of chewed up twenty-five cent gumballs—the white ones.

In this timeline, I got a dick that gets hard, and a car I didn't borrow from my mom, and I tell funny jokes at the right times. This procedure might not get me all the way there, but I pray it could get me through what I'm thinking will be the hardest part.

I see a sign that says "Roland, Oklahoma City Limits." So that's where I am. Midnight in the middle of nowhere, rolled over in Roland, Oklahoma. An occasional car zips by. I consider jumping in front of one. I'm trying to muster the courage and thinking about how my mom will be better off that way. I put together a few steps and fall down on the shoulder. I see a patient nail in the road, just a few inches on the other side of the white line. I wonder what'll happen first, me gathering the energy to roll into the street or the nail destroying a tire. I try to assert myself. I look right at the nail.

"Fuck you, nail," I say defiantly. "You think you can do damage? You're a nail. I'm a man, full of bones."

The nail, unimpressed, doesn't blink. It stands on its head, mocking me, with a look that says, "I can do this forever, *amigo.*"

I can't do this forever. Time is slow and passing it, the way I am now, is agonizing. If you've ever not known how you are going to continue living inside your head, wishing each breath could be your last, but you know it won't be unless you do something about it, hoping your life will flash before your eyes, not because you care to rehash everything, just because that's what you've heard happens before you die and you'd welcome the end, you'd know the experience is enough to cause your rational mind to pick up anchor and sail away. When addiction is the cause of all your troubles, the worst part about experiencing the worst part of your life over and over again is knowing that next time it'll be worse. It's kind of like that song that goes, *I'll love you more today than yesterday, but not as much as tomorrow.* Just replace "love you more" with "hate myself and want to die."

I can't scream for help. I can't muster the strength, but I also don't want it because I know help would not bring more drugs. I am out of what I need to keep me going, hundreds of miles from someone I know, puking out the side of my mouth, wishing I could be a nail in the road instead of myself. I hold my breath as long as I can. I don't last long. I exhale. I suck air back in, this time determined to pass out.

Faces of the people I've known pass by, but they're moving too fast. No memories, not even moments—just faces zipping through my mind's eye. I breathe and my eyes adjust and the sun is out. It's daytime, and I'm still in the road. A car zooms by, like the faces. The nail looks like it moved a few inches closer to the middle of the road.

I look beyond the nail, to the other side of the street. There's a backpack in the grass. I can't fucking believe it. This John Prine enthusiast stole everything except what I wanted to keep. If he was here right now, I'd hug him before I take a swing and miss. I run across the street and lift the backpack out of the grass. Only, it's not a backpack. It's a trash bag. Whatever spirit I have left flies out of my body. I stare at the dirt and asphalt, dejected. I walk back across the road. A car zooms by and almost hits me. I stand there for a second, head down. I hear laughing so I look up. It's the nail. "Look both ways, dumb ass."

"Can't you see I'm trying to get hit, you rusty, glorified pushpin?"

I think about the fifth grade. That's before experiences turned me inside out. I remember the New Testament story of Lazarus coming back from the dead. I went to Catholic school, and they taught us the Bible was not meant to be taken literally, even the Gospels — at least some of the more enlightened teachers did. I wonder how this story came about. What inspired it? If Lazarus did exist, what did Jesus do to wake him up? I wonder if Lazarus was so dead that his soul, or his mind, left his body.

The dehydration puts me back on the ground, and my face burns on the hot road. I hear the sprinklers turn on in the field next to me. I decide to try rolling into the field. Maybe I'll be able to get some water on my face, cool off a bit. This will take everything I have. I manage to move. Every time I roll I hit another rock. I roll again and again onto these big rocks in the field. I feel them moving around under my back. My heart pumps so fast I think it might hop out my throat and onto the asphalt, twitch like a just run over and about to die small animal. My pores feel like sores all over my body, and the sweat is painful to pass. I know that sounds crazy, that sweat can hurt, but sniff a brick of heroin every day for a few months then chain yourself to the bedpost. You'll see.

With every roll toward the field I have another wish. *Roll.* A car to run me over, please. *Roll.* Maybe a tractor. *Roll.* Or a rogue cow to trample me. *Roll.* Lightning. Smite me, Jesus. It'll be kinder than what you did for Lazarus. *Roll.* Are there are alligators in Oklahoma?

Finally, I make it into the field. I realize I have made a terrible mistake. I am now on the rain forest floor. I feel so small in that field. None of the water makes it to me, but I can feel the humidity. The canopy of whatever is growing in the field will not allow a single drop to land on my face or in my mouth. And now the bugs come. Ants and mosquitoes start to pick at me. I am decomposing, but quite sure I'm still alive, unfortunately. They are relentless, driving me insane—no, more insane. I bury my face in cow shit and dirt. I hold my breath and wait. Sweat continues to fire out of me. This is it, I think. I'm going to die with my face in shit. Around the minute mark I can't stop myself from sucking in whatever oxygen I can find in the soil. I can still hear that fucking nail laughing at me. I don't know what is growing in this field. I don't even know in what kind of field I'll die. If I could just get whatever the fuck is poking me in the back out from under me, maybe that will allow my brain to turn off.

I can't take it. I put my hand behind my back to remove the rocks from under me. I feel damp material. It's familiar. It's my fucking backpack. This find gives me a bit of energy. I roll the pack off my shoulders and out from under me. I put it in front of me and army crawl forward, like a horse following a carrot.

I manage to pull the bag open and find a bundle of dope, and wouldn't you know it, a rolled-up dollar bill. I rip open the bags and pour them onto my copy of *On the Road.* I know. Give me a break. I'm on the road and people who like to pretend to read are impressed by it.

Sniff. I hope I don't get hit by a fucking car. *Sniff.* Or mangled by a wandering cow. *Sniff.* Jesus, you've saved me. *Sniff.* Are there alligators in Oklahoma?

Slack in the line. Throttle down. My heartbeat slows to a march, then a fifth-grade slow dance. My breathing just about matches the arrhythmic traffic. The bug racket is harmony. The mosquito hordes sparkle in the tall grass. I am the faintest bit of this Oklahoma wilderness. I better get up and move before I fall asleep in the field. I stand and realize a few things. It's a corn field. And Lazarus must have been an addict. Oh, my Lord, was Jesus a dealer? Is that it? Maybe I'll go back to school again, theology this time.

I put my thumb out. A little time passes, and someone slows down. But as they pull toward the side of the road, I sense impending danger. I hold my hands up, signaling for them to stop. I pick up that cunt of a nail and launch him into the cow shit.

A MIDWESTERN PURGATORY

HEATHER LANG-CASSERA

The night that I saw Charlie the dog in the corner of my living room had been, up until that point, no different than most other nights. It was 2 a.m., and insomnia had struck. I thought, *Maybe if I go pee, I'll be able to fall asleep.* Mind you, I had already tried the ol' empty-the-bladder trick two, three, and then four times that night. But anything felt better than staring at the dark ceiling of my rural farmhouse counting down the hours until I had to unwrap myself from the comforts of my quilt for the day. Once awake, I knew I would have to shiver until the warm water could reach the showerhead. Typically, this only took a minute or two, but when the temperatures were subzero and the sun was still tucked in somewhere beyond the Midwest horizon, it often felt like an entire lifetime.

During the era of the Charlie-the-dog sighting, I lived in a rural Wisconsin village. You know the type: The ones where you can hear the church bells regardless of where you live in town—even if you aren't much of one for religion. Relief from those hourly clatters-and-chimes came only in the night. They were, for me, however, replaced by a ticking clock, one of chronic insomnia.

In the winter, I had two wake-up times. First, I had to rise to see if it had snowed. Waking at 4 a.m., I allotted two hours for snow-shoveling activity. If I needed more time, which happened more than once, I was out of luck (which is *bad* when you're the opening technician in the village's only veterinary clinic). The second wake-up time was 6 a.m., a gift from the Wisconsin snow deities—*if* they had decided to spare me that day.

If it had snowed, I needed to shovel the driveway so that I could get to work. And, I needed to shovel the sidewalk in order to avoid another hefty fine from the village. These activities occurred after the shower and between at least two rounds of much-needed light roast coffee, the kind with the most caffeine.

I'd broken four shovels that season, and each time I'd stake the wrecked tool into the snowbank in front of my house. For each broken shovel, I'd offer up a moment of silence. These weren't so much ceremonies of remembrance. Rather, they were born of utter frustration. Despite not having much of a temper, after having shoveled for an hour in the dark and frigid air, and having to soon head off to work for a ten-hour shift with still-frozen feet, the broken shovels made me want to ... well, they made me want to break something. Nevertheless, during these moments, I'd recoup and remind myself that shoveling was good exercise, or something.

My ex was the one who had owned the truck, the type of hearty vehicle that can, you know, handle a front plow.

I'd watch my neighbors layer their snow in a tidy corner of each driveway. Of course, they had big-tired, all-wheel pickup trucks—or whatever it is that makes a truck impressive—and on the front they'd mounted plows. Quickly, they'd removed the majority of their snow and then cleaned up the perimeter using hand-held shovels with the seeming ease of tying a bow on a holiday gift. I always hoped they'd offer to do a quick pass along my stretch, but never once did it happen. *So much for small-town friendliness*, I thought.

But this wasn't entirely their fault. Before he moved out, my husband hadn't exactly been a beacon of warmth to the neighbors. You know that guy who'd yell, "Get off my lawn!" Yup, that guy, but the early thirties version. Of course, it wasn't entirely his fault that we hadn't bonded with the neighbors. While I pleaded with him not to cause a scene, I didn't exactly counter his actions by knocking on the neighbors' doors with friendly gestures; I never came up with excuses to say "Hello!" like borrowing sugar or bringing back homemade chocolate chip cookies or whatever it was that I should have done right.

Since my husband had moved out, I had to prioritize the numerous chores around the house. The home needed a lot of care— largely because it was old, so old that no one knew exactly when it had been built. The upstairs, which housed all the bedrooms, had no heating system, only square holes covered by antique vents—gravity registers, I believe they were called—that allowed the warmer downstairs air to rise more naturally. Some days, it was as if the Wisconsin winter cackled at the gentleness of this system. The wind would whisper through the leaky, wooden walls. From its piecemeal structure, it was clear that the home had been built in stages. Perhaps one portion was the original farmhouse and another a tacked-on living room. Increasingly, after moving in, the sliding wooden doors made me think of an old-fashioned in-home funeral parlor.

Because it was even colder upstairs, and because I was the only one living in the two-story home, I slept in a room on the main floor, the one with the sliding wooden doors—largely because I could. The marriage had been short, only one year together and another legally while trying to get divorced. "What a wild mistake!" an acquaintance would later tell me. Regardless of its length, the marriage had been difficult for both of us, and it felt good to choose my own bedtimes—and bedroom—and to leave my books in piles as I pleased, and to do the dishes as loudly as I wanted. And, to not have to tiptoe around another's schedule ... or heart.

Anyhow, the night that I saw Charlie the dog, I had been lying awake at two-something a.m. wondering if it would snow sometime over the next couple of hours. My mind had shifted to anesthesia calculations—not exactly counting sheep. Despite my degree in the Liberal Arts, I had since worked to earn my license as a Certified Veterinary Technician. Having never been of the math and science side of the brain, this was a rewarding accomplishment, but sometimes I worried that others would find me out, tell me that I should be writing copy or slinging coffee instead of administering and monitoring anesthesia and the like. My insecurities, however, made me particularly cautious. I told myself this was an asset. That, in the end, whatever led me to be so meticulous must have, ultimately, been positive.

Not wanting to go down that obnoxious path in my brain in the middle of the night, the one that thought about work while I should be sleeping, I dragged myself out of my old oak bed and to the bathroom, which was just around the corner. It was my fifth if-I-empty-my-bladder-then-maybe-I'll-be-able-to-fall-asleep   attempt that night. But as soon as my foot crossed the interior threshold of the heavy wooden sliding doors, I saw him.

There, in the corner of my living room, appeared to be a scraggly, overweight dachshund mix—one that had arrived at the veterinary clinic just minutes after I had gotten to work the day before. It was Charlie. The dog. From work. In my living room. In the middle of the night. And *that* was impossible. Not just highly improbable. It was literally impossible that Charlie could be sitting in my living room, or anywhere for that matter.

Charlie had been an established patient at the veterinary office. He was loyal to his mom (his owner), yet loving, almost jovial, with each member of the clinic staff. His curiosity was admirable, and, no matter how his hair was groomed, it seemed as if—within a week— his shaggy bangs would once again block his view of the world. Easily distracted by both milk bones and soft treats, Charlie might have been even more food motivated than I was. (And, this was quite the feat.) In fact, the only thing greater than 1.) his love for his owner and 2.) his adoration of food may have been his waistline.

That morning—the morning *before* I saw Charlie in my living room—the dog had arrived at the clinic in severe pain. He'd had a bad back for some time by then, and his owner was working toward his shedding a few pounds. Charlie was also on activity restrictions— nothing too serious, but he wasn't supposed to jump on and off furniture, nor was he to be around the other, much larger, dogs. That morning, however, the worst-case scenario had happened. Charlie had escaped his baby-gated section of the house and, in a moment of barks and excitement, he'd been trampled by one of the happy-go-lucky Labrador retrievers who lived beneath the same roof. Charlie's already injured spine was in shambles.

Once they arrived at the clinic, we injected high-end doses of synthetic opioids. But nothing touched the piercing pain. The only ones who might have been able to help him were at the veterinary teaching hospital, which was one hour away. It was possible that, for thousands of dollars for a nerve-related surgery, a procedure with a discouragingly low success rate, Charlie's spine might have—just maybe—healed. Like many who lived in that small town within which I worked, the pet owner had very little money. Out of compassion, the woman elected to put Charlie to rest.

I was *that* technician, the one who cried at every euthanasia. A few owners were annoyed at my unprofessionalism, more took comfort in the company of another's tears, and many couldn't care less either way. Regardless, I couldn't help it. The tears were visceral, involuntary. Sometimes I could wait until after I'd left the room, but no matter what, they'd always come.

Charlie's passing, however, landed in my heart in an even more trying way. This was because, I thought that maybe, just maybe, I could be the one to save him. *I could drive the dog into the city*, I thought, *and put the surgery fees on my own credit card. I just might have enough room.* Really, though, the decision wasn't mine to make. Or, was it? I still don't know.

There's something that's been on my mind over the past few years. I've talked to family members at holidays, friends on nights out, and colleagues at writing events about something I can only call *the moment*, or, perhaps, *"the moment of no return."* It seems that, when it comes right down to it, everything in life is about a single thing—an action, a phrase, a decision or lack thereof, or maybe we don't even know what it is, but it punches us in the gut. It's not always something like love at first sight. No, oftentimes moments mark an end. Sometimes the moment is subtle.

When it comes to relationships, it sometimes occurs long before the breakup. One friend told me that, for her, she knew it was over when she was quietly—cheerfully—singing to herself on a long flight home from a friend's wedding, and her boyfriend asked her, albeit nicely, to stop. She broke into tears. Another friend admitted that he knew it was over when his boyfriend wore a pair of shoes that he just couldn't stand. Surely, this moment was symptomatic of something greater, my friend admits. And, the significant other never knew; in fact, they stayed together for another two years. *Because who breaks up over shoes?*

What was the *"the moment of no return"* for my marriage? Well, I'm not so sure that I know anymore. Or, maybe, even now, five years later, I just don't want to admit it, not even to myself. This is because it might have been the very moment that he popped the question. At an Italian restaurant, with a beautiful blue ring, my then-boyfriend asked me to marry him. I said, "yes," of course, but a week later I mustered the courage to ask, "Why blue?" These words climbed from my throat. I had hoped to hear, *Because blue is your favorite color, silly.* This is what I had heard in my head as I practiced asking him that question again and again. Instead, however, without looking at me, my new fiancé haphazardly replied with something like this, "Because it's blue! It matches your eyes." Here's the thing, though. My eyes are hazel. *Maybe* green. My response? Well, I didn't say a word. I didn't know how.

Here's a moment, though, one about which I'm much more certain: the beginning of the end of my career as a veterinary technician. It was the moment that I saw Charlie the dog sitting in my living room, seemingly alive, on a dark winter night. I knew that the quirky and loveable pooch, the kind soul whose pain we had taken away earlier that day, whose heart had been silent when I had placed my stethoscope against his chest, could not actually be there looking at me. However, I also know that I saw him there in my house that night. He seemed okay, comfortable actually. And, I was not afraid. The entire exchange felt surprisingly matter of fact. He looked at me. I looked at him. I went to the bathroom, not even closing the door, and when I came back out, he was gone. But I knew that my days in veterinary medicine were numbered. There's something about "seeing" a dead dog that changes a person.

Could I have saved Charlie? What about my marriage? That night, after I saw Charlie, I looked out the window at my broken shovels—whose own splintered spines reached toward the sky—and I remembered that I was the one who had broken them. Nevertheless, that night, the snow deities took pity on me, and they let me sleep that two extra hours.

SNAPPED!

June 11th, 2019
Dixon Place | New York City

Podcast Episode 49

"July 1995"
written by Kent D. Wolf
and performed by Naomi Gordon-Loebl

"Snapped! Reflection"
written by Mike Dressel

JULY 1995

KENT D. WOLF

"You gotta understand, son, the anus is a one-way chute. That's just basic anatomy," my dad says to me from the driver's seat, in between sips of Old Milwaukee Light. Next to him is my 27-year-old half-brother, who has just outed me to my parents. I am nineteen years old.

"You know, when I was in the Air Force, I could've been court-martialed for having anal intercourse with my wife," my brother says, and all I want to ask him is, "Why? When you found that magazine in my room, why didn't you come to me first? You knew what would happen. What would happen to *me.*"

Instead, I stay silent in the backseat of the family car, which sits parked on our overgrown lawn. We're not headed anywhere, and for that I should feel grateful—as my dad is prone to driving drunk along the back roads that snake around our Illinois farm, but I would gladly give him a lifetime's worth of beer to drive me away from here.

The muggy stillness of a July night blankets the car, but from inside the house my mother's voice tears through it. She has—for lack of a better word—snapped. Days earlier she had major surgery on her crumbling spine and was confined to bed. Now she's shuffling back and forth in front of her rented hospital bed, pulling at her hair, screaming. It is a wordless curse. At God. At this pox on her family. At me.

Earlier that afternoon, pulling into the driveway after a visit with a friend, I found her hobbling in circles in front of the garage, muttering to herself, eyes wild, one hand pressed gingerly to her lower back. I'd barely stepped out of the car when she grabbed my wrists, telling me that I was sick, would have to drop out of college and be admitted to one of those pray-away-the-gay reparative therapy programs.

I was tempted to lie to her, to deny what months earlier I had come to accept, if only to preserve my freedom and my future. "Is it true?" she asked. "Yes," I said, with a surprising amount of conviction.

My mom and her anger are why I'm now confined to the car with my dad. It's the only peaceful place he can talk to me, and we're here to discuss whether or not they'll allow me to leave the farm. In less than three days I'm scheduled to fly from Chicago to Buenos Aires for my junior year abroad. I tell myself to be quiet and let my dad talk, but I can't stop the panic creeping up my throat like bile. I have no car, no place of my own. What little money I have was earned earlier that summer from trimming rows of growing Christmas trees with a machete. Every few trees I would have to stop and pry the blade from my shin guard when my arm slipped on the downswing. I'd worked clumsily, hastily, to pull further ahead of the guys who shouted "faggot!" at me from the neighboring rows in between swings of their own blades. The promise of escape to another continent had kept me going. In the dark of the car neither my dad nor my brother see the plane ticket pressed to my chest like a talisman.

For me there is nothing idyllic about farm life. It is lonely, for me at least, for I am different even if I haven't articulated it to those around me. The boys with the machetes know it. My mom knows it, too, as the only question she asks every time she phones me at college is, "Do you have a girlfriend yet?" If she'd asked about a potential boyfriend instead, the answer, sadly, would've been the same. I am one of a handful of out students at my small liberal arts college, and my life on campus is almost as lonely as life on the farm. Just when my real life feels like it's finally set to begin — in a big city in faraway country, like a kind of fairy tale — it may all end up being taken away from me here in the car with my dad.

In the car my dad is in his element, loosened up by liquor and addressing a captive audience. As far back as I can remember, my father has absolutely *lived* to tell stories. He's a yarn spinner, a slinger of anecdotes and random facts, an even folksier Garrison Keillor with a penchant for intentionally mispronouncing words for added folksiness.

"Son, when I picture your future, all see is a brick wall," he says. "It's a sad life, that one, and let me tell ya why. When I was a senior

148

in high school, my pal Gail and I took a used car out for a test drive. Picture it, I'm behind the wheel, cruising along, enjoying the breeze, the Everly Brothers on the radio, when all of a sudden the salesman reaches over and grabs my you-know-what. Before I can pry his grubby mitt off me, my buddy Gail's springing up from the backseat like lightning and locks his arm around the guy's neck so hard he 'bout near chokes to death. You see what kind of people they are, these PuhVERTs?"

He looks for me in the rearview mirror, but it is too dark for him to see me. Still, I give him the slightest of nods.

"And you know what happened to that no-good creep? Not long after, a fella out fishing for bluegill found his body floatin' face down in the canal. It's the town's one and only murder and to this day nobody knows who did it. A real tragedy, that one," he says with a shake of his head.

My dad is not the aggressor in his tale, nor is he one to wish death upon anyone, but the apparent moral of his story unsettles me. Was death what the car salesman deserved? Is this the fate that awaits me? To be preyed upon by older men? Or will I one day do the preying? I shift uncomfortably in my seat.

"That's the kinda guy you need to watch out for, son. They're everywhere," he says. "Did I ever tell you about my time undercover?"

For over twenty years my dad has worked as an Illinois State Trooper. He speaks of his job rarely, as most days he issues tickets to speeders and toll evaders. All I know about his time as a detective is his inability to grow a convincing mustache thanks to a scar on his upper lip from a motorcycle accident when he was sixteen.

"Well, at the time we didn't know it was John Wayne Gacy, but young men were disappearing up by Chicago, and we were under pressure to find the guy behind it. For months the sergeant had me hanging in the men's toilets at the rest stops off the tollway. I'd stand around for hours in those stinkin' stalls waiting for guys to creep up on me so I could arrest 'em. Your old dad shouldn't even tell you some of the nasty things these puhVERTs wanted to do to me, but I swear to ya, son, one of 'em said to me, oh I get sick just thinkin' about it, he said he was gonna put his tongue in my asshole, can you believe that?"

His eyes look for mine again in the rearview mirror. The message is clear: The gay lifestyle is one of violence and depravity. Of filthy toilets and filthy acts. Of missing boys and shallow graves.

"That's what's waiting for you, my boy, and it scares me to death. And I haven't even mentioned AIDS. It's a death sentence. I mean, I can't see you making it to the age of 25. It breaks my heart. So now tell me, how can we let you go halfway 'round the world, knowing all this?" he says.

I set down my plane ticket next to me. I'm afraid the sweat from my hands will smear the ink and make the ticket useless. "You'll just have to trust me, I guess?"

"I tell ya what, you're going to make me a promise. A promise from a son to his dad, okay? Promise me that you won't try anything. You won't go to any bars. You won't congregate with homosexuals. Stay away from all that stuff and you can get on the plane. Do we have a deal?" he says.

I don't spend a second mulling over his offer. "Yes, Dad, we have a deal. I promise," I say.

With that, he tells me to head to bed, and I slip into the house as quietly as possible.

My father, despite his own disappointment and revulsion, is setting me free, but I still owe someone a pound of flesh. My mother carries with her an insurmountable trauma. How this came to be is her story to tell, not mine, but what I can tell you is that from this pain she wounds just as deeply as she loves. Over the years I have learned to keep my guard up, my heart closed, but even when I can see the blade coming, it always finds its mark. In the warm moments, when her love is the softest, most comforting thing, I tend to forgive her this volatility, but the words she burns me with the following morning will make a hole so deep in my heart it will never fully heal.

I wake early. Our rooster has made sure of it, but my sleep was a fitful one anyway, as I could hear my parents arguing through the night about my father's decision. When I turn over, I see her. My mother. I don't know how long she's been standing next to my bed, how long she's been waiting for me to open my eyes.

"When I woke up this morning, I thought to myself, 'Everything's going to be alright,'" she says flatly. "But you know what? It won't ever be. I hate you. In fact, I wish you had never been born." Her eyes are cold and empty, but there is a hint of a smile on her face. Does she find this funny? No, she's wearing a smirk of satisfaction, one that says, "Now you hurt, too," and with that, her job is done. She leaves the room and I wonder if I still have a mother. Two days later I am on a plane.

.

"SNAPPED!" REFLECTION

MIKE DRESSEL
"SNAPPED!" HOST AND FOUNDING MEMBER

There is an ever-expanding Google Doc where we keep potential themes for *No, YOU Tell It!* shows, but none felt right for our event with Lambda Literary in 2019. I brainstormed some new options and emailed them to Kelly Jean in the early stages of planning our inaugural Pride month edition of *NYTI*. After weighing and jettisoning the likes of "Rites" (a little dull) and "All Tea, No Sympathy," (a little too clever), we settled on "Snapped!"

In designing a *No, YOU Tell It!* show, we aim for a theme with a little elasticity, some oxygen around the idea, one that is as open to writerly interpretation as possible. When I suggested "Snapped!" I was thinking it could work along the lines of "that song snapped," i.e., it was good, per the slang, and snapped like sassy finger percussion, a sign of approval or an aural punctuation mark, but also as in "they have had it!" — they've lost it, hit their limit, snapped! — because, truly, by the summer of 2019, many of us had indeed had it. With the continued fallout of the 2016 election, the repeated erosion of civil liberties, with attacks on BIPOC communities, with trans persons under threat of violence and a spate of "bathroom bills" trying to police gender expression, the national mood was one of sustained dread for anyone who wasn't cisgender, straight, white, and male. It began to feel like no matter how many gains were made, there were always forces keen to stick their thumb on the scale of justice or to rollback any advances.

Those struggles generated a persistent static running underneath the summer of 2019, as New York City prepared to play host to WorldPride for the first time. It coincided with the 50th Anniversary of the Stonewall Riots, the first volley in the national fight for gay rights. It felt both essential to celebrate queer history and progress and also as if we might be gearing up for battle once again. But as evidenced by the legacy of Stonewall, and the AIDS activism of the 80s and 90s, and the more recent fight for marriage equality, queer people excel at dual purposes: We can march in the morning and carouse into the night; we mobilize and then we socialize. It's glitter and combat boots, hon.

I thought we could use the *NYTI* platform to be a small part of what was happening in New York that June—a diverse mix of concerts, readings, lectures, performances, and parties. It was with these upcoming celebrations in mind that we proposed the co-branded storytelling event to Lambda Literary. It was my hope that our particular format for embodying and presenting stories would be a unique "in" for the audience to lived, queer experiences. Above all, I wanted to be included, in some small way, to contribute to what seemed like an important moment.

The cohort of queer storytellers assembled for "Snapped!" included a performer/educator/raconteur, two Lambda Literary Fellows, and literary agent and Lambda Literary board member Kent D. Wolf. It was a big ask to have Kent switch roles, as he's usually the one shepherding other writers' projects. Now, he was being tasked with writing, editing, and sharing his own unique story.

When pitching the idea, I wrote that I hoped we could feature stories not solely of "coming out," but ones that offered additional complexity in the representation of queer lives, to feature pieces ranging from gay marriage to gay divorce, on polyamory and PrEP; that as a queer community, we're not always in lockstep, and there are complex issues that circle around race, class, and values. The coming out story became one of the hallmarks of queer expression, and in recent years there have been heartwarming YouTube videos and TikToks, in addition to a trove of literature dedicated to the subject. And it should by no means be devalued.

Coming out is a first step, and a process that one revisits many times over with friends, family, coworkers, and others—an exhibition of the courage and vulnerability it takes to eschew the closet for something authentic. Still, the coming out story has become a trope, the oft-expected narrative. They can come across as a little too "feel good" and polished, and I was interested in stories that were more jagged and complicated, imperfect.

In hindsight I hoped perhaps a theme like "Snapped!" was a way into a more complicated, and less comfortable narrative space. What Kent brought to the table in response to the theme is in part what makes his piece so arresting. It's not about coming out but being outed — in this case to his family at the age of nineteen — and to be outed puts that person in a defensive position. It requires a different set of calibrations: deny, confirm, or hedge. Rather than an instigation, it's the fallout.

"July 1995" begins with an inversion, a queering of traditional father-son "birds and bees" talk that would play as a near-parody if the scenario weren't absolutely excruciating. "You gotta understand, son, the anus is a one-way chute. That's just basic anatomy," the narrator's father, cradling an open can of beer, tells him as they sit side-by-side in the confines of his automobile. The alcohol-abetted cautionary tales of the homosexual lifestyle continue, informed by his time undercover as an Illinois state trooper:

"For months the sergeant had me hanging in the men's toilets at the rest stops off the tollway. I'd stand around for hours in those stinkin' stalls waiting for guys to creep up on me so I could arrest 'em. Your old dad shouldn't even tell you some of the nasty things these puhVERTs wanted to do to me, but I swear to ya, son, one of 'em said to me, oh I get sick just thinkin' about it, he said he was gonna put his tongue in my asshole, can you believe that?"

What perpetuates the tension of the story is wondering how far the narrator will sublimate his identity to get what he most desperately wants, an escape from the isolation of Midwestern farm life that lies in the form of a plane ticket for a semester abroad in South America, his negotiation for autonomy. Despite the story's premise, it is not the narrator who snaps in this piece, or his father, with his beery warnings and ultimately grudging acceptance, it's his mother, whose response is an anger that is almost inscrutable. "I'd barely stepped out of the car," Kent writes of his encounter with her earlier that day, "when she grabbed my wrists, telling me that I was sick, would have to drop out of college and be admitted to one of those pray-away-the-gay reparative-therapy programs." Again, the story flips certain expectations, as it's often the mother in the role of ally, the father as disappointed figure.

The title itself is a reminder of where we were two-and-a-half decades ago, situating the reader chronologically, if subtly, both far from 2022 while illustrating the same ostracization, stereotypes, and debunked science used against queer people still. Speaking as someone who grew up a contemporary of Kent's, it's a reminder of the time of "Don't Ask, Don't Tell" and the Defense of Marriage Act—Clinton era political compromises that kept queer people as second-class citizens. It calls to mind Pedro Zamora, who brought AIDS awareness into Gen X households on MTV's "The Real World" and died of the disease a year prior. In 1995 antiretroviral therapy, or "the AIDS cocktail," was recognized by the FDA, a breakthrough which meant HIV was no longer seen as an immediate death sentence.

Kent posted on social media in June of 2021 that "[t]wo years ago this Pride month I wrote an essay about a painful memory I carried with me for 25 years. Words can wound but they also have the capacity to heal." I think that idea speaks to his personal experience and to so much of the work of storytelling overall, at least in the way *No, YOU Tell It!* approaches it. If you can articulate your story, you've gained a measure of control over it. Pain isn't erased, but it can be contended with, understood. We presented "Snapped!" on a warm June evening in the Lounge at Dixon Place on the Lower East Side, the packed audience scattered around the funky rec room furniture. Whether it was the general mood across the five boroughs, the synergy of the performers, or possibly even my charming event hosting, the night turned out as well as we intended. Our event may have been more humble compared to some of the high profile celebrity performances taking place that month, but that didn't mean it was any less impactful. We received snaps of approval from the audience. And while that evening itself was ephemeral, the stories we presented had an afterlife. As Kent's reflection illustrates, they persist in the minds of the author and audience, on the podcast and beyond. Hopefully, you find a measure of solace from the struggle as you read "July 1995."

a M U S E

September 17th, 2019
The Astoria Bookshop | Queens

Podcast Episode 52

"The Neighbor's Muse"
written by H.E. Fisher
and performed by Ellie Dvorkin Dunn

"Fun"
written by Ellie Dvorkin Dunn
and performed by H.E. Fisher

Kelly Jean Fitzsimmons | Series Creator and Producer

.

No, YOU Tell It! offers a strange and extraordinary alchemy to stories that allow the author—and audiences—to go inside the mind of the reader; it is a kind of delicious translation. NYTI reader-performers are not "cast" against "type" per se, but in a way that adds a fresh point of view and dimension to each written piece. —storyteller, H.E. Fisher

I've seen the word alchemy—the seemingly magical process of transformation, creation, or combination—used more than once to describe *No, YOU Tell It!* As the woman behind the curtain who spends countless hours on scheduling, grant applications, and social media posts, the words "seemingly magical" make me want to both laugh and cry.

Our "aMuse" show came from a practical combination of elements. It was our first Bookend Event for the Brooklyn Book Festival—a series of literary events that take place across the five boroughs leading up to the festival. I produced this Queens-based Bookend Event with support from the first grant awarded to us by the Queens Council on the Arts. My idea of having poets and comedians trade tales aligned with our grant proposal by pushing artists outside their lanes to strengthen their craft while expanding their creative network. As a producer, I also hoped the fun literary angle would make our Bookend Event stand out, attracting new audience members through the festival website.

When adding storytellers into the mix, I immediately thought of Ellie Dvorkin Dunn, an alum *NYTI* storyteller and one of my all-time favorite comedic performers. I reached out to poet and multi-genre writer H.E. Fisher because while I'd loved the lyrical eloquence of her words for over a decade, the show gave us the chance to finally meet in person. Everything was coming together exactly as I planned, but I've produced *No, YOU Tell It!* long enough to know to expect the unexpected.

Ellie contacted me privately with concerns that she'd drafted a deeply personal, emotional, and heavy story instead of one filled with punchlines. As the Queens-representing comedian, she feared she was wasting an opportunity to flex her humor muscles. I'll admit that when tossing ingredients into my show cauldron, I imagined Ellie spicing up the night with laughter. Still, I wanted her to embrace this story that she clearly needed to tell. I encouraged her to stick with the draft, reminding her that she might swap with someone whose story had funny elements, and she could elicit laughter from the audience that way.

Enter her story partner H.E. Fisher's fantastic tale about a dyed-in-wool New Yorker facing unforeseen suburban awkwardness after moving to a residential area. Ellie and I meticulously rehearsed getting the voice just right for the peculiar new neighbor, Mrs. Weaver, described as having "a somewhat deflated tone as though the air had been let out a bit and she needed pumping." Our efforts paid off as Ellie not only made the audience laugh but also transported us out of The Astoria Bookshop's intimate setting into the bizarre discomfort of negotiating neighborly encounters.

When Fisher and I rehearsed Ellie's "aMuse" story, we faced a different challenge. The narrative bounces between an adult narrator who doesn't find anything amusing about her lifelong role as forced caretaker of her gambling-addicted mother and the childlike perspective of a kid tagging along for a day at the slots in Atlantic City. The song "On the Radio" by Donna Summer provides a vital hinge point between the two timelines. Prompting Fisher to ask me, "Should I sing it?"

We practiced her singing with a light touch. But on the night, Fisher went for it! Her emotional delivery manifested a palpable nostalgia felt by everyone in the bookshop. So much so, that the second time Fisher sang out,

On the radio.

The audience joined in, accompanying her with:

Whoa, oh, oh on the radio!

Everyone was held together in that moment of song, a seemingly magical moment that only existed because of hours and hours of work. Still, there is no denying the mystical element of combining people who may not have ever met otherwise and helping them to step into each other's stories. Ellie describes it this way:

> *I, a comedian, unwittingly used the poetry of a pop song to drive my dramatic story home, and H.E. Fisher, a poet, used her comedic perspective to create a piece worthy of a stand-up routine. This is the "alchemy" of No, YOU Tell It! that Fisher refers to, and this magic is the reason I say a wholehearted "yes" every time.*

THE NEIGHBOR'S MUSE

H.E. FISHER

Dan and I were throwing dinner together when the doorbell rang. After twenty years of living with dysfunctional New York City buzzers, the actual sound of an alarmingly standardized *ding-dong* was startling. I went downstairs to see who it was—trying not to trip on all the packing boxes lining the hallway—and automatically put one eye up to the door to look through the peephole. There wasn't one. I had to wonder: Was it really that safe here in the suburbs? I took my chances and opened the door. A high-pitched, pasteurized voice leapt out at me from a man with dark round eyes and thick black eyebrows that seemed to shuttle up and down in time to an invisible neurological beat.

"We're the Weavers! Welcome to the neighborhood!" he said.

He was with a woman with short, permed brown hair, and a young boy with static, almost frozen features.

My five-year-old son came racing down the stairs.

"Who is it, Mom?"

"Neighbors, I think."

"Neighbors?" he said dubiously.

"Who is *this*?" Mr. Weaver said, referring to our son with such over-the-top enthusiasm I expected him to honk his nose and squeeze a bike horn.

"Our oldest," I said, instinctively putting my arm around him.

"Well, *hello!*"

Mr. Weaver spoke as though he had studied a handbook on how to conduct social interactions. CHAPTER ONE: THE ART OF GREETING NEIGHBORS.

Our son said nothing and ran back upstairs.

Mr. Weaver introduced his family. "This is Ronnie," he said gesturing to the boy. "I am Lewis, and this is my wife Joanie."

"Joan," she corrected him firmly, but in a somewhat deflated tone as though the air had been let out a bit and she needed pumping.

Dan joined me at the door and had the courteous wherewithal to invite the Weavers in. Lewis immediately assaulted Dan with

Weaver facts—I thought I detected the words *"shoe repair"* —and then marched right past us, bounding up the hallway stairs to the living room. Joan and son followed.

"Are you liking it here so far?" Joan asked, and before I could respond added, "Well, of course you only just got here, but you *will* like it."

"Thank you," I said, trying to remember what part of the dinner process we were in. "I think the oven is on."

Joan followed me into the kitchen.

"Oh, look how nice," she said, commenting on the décor. "So different from ours."

I knew our kids had to be hungry, and I also knew there'd be no way to get them to eat while guests were in the house. What person with kids drops by at dinnertime? *This* was the nightmare ... The suburbs. I arrived kicking and screaming. I'd had concerns all along: Would *The Times* deliver here? Would the supermarket have vegetarian chicken salad? Would I be a fashion pariah if I wore black all the time? Would I fit in? Would I *want* to?

We had felt a desperate pull to leave the city: the air was bad, our baby girl and I were getting nosebleeds, and I was diagnosed with asthma. We moved almost a year to the day after the Towers fell—part of the post-9/11 diaspora.

"How old are the children?" Joan asked. She wasn't making eye contact with me.

"Two and five," I told her.

"Ronnie is five! The boys will be starting kindergarten together. That's nice." She was looking at something near my left ear.

"Cool," I said, flicking my eyes in my left ear's direction in an effort to wrangle her gaze and wrestle it back to my own. Instead, Joan's eyes locked onto a point somewhere over my right shoulder.

"I'd love for you to see how I've decorated," she said.

Apparently, Joan was also a student of the HUMAN BEHAVIOR HANDBOOK. *CHAPTER TWO: CHIT-CHATTING WITH NEW NEIGHBORS. Repeat after me: How old are your children? I'd love for you to see how I've decorated! Gee, are you liking it here?* I felt a pang. I'd always cherished the informal, unfiltered way New Yorkers talked to one another. One time, on the N train, a young woman sitting next to me looked at me and squirming in her seat said, "I think I have a vaginal infection." I gave the her the name of my gynecologist.

"C'mon, I'll show you our house," Joan said, boldly going down the steps to the front door. "Lewis and your husband can watch the kids."

"You mean *now*?" I asked.

She went out. I mumbled something to Dan—and followed her a few doors down to her home. Joan went inside without using a key.

"You leave the door unlocked?" I asked, scandalized, and stepped inside behind her.

Joan's eyes fell to the floor, transfixed on a single white tile. "We do." She seemed to be considering the question further. "You'll get used to this life," she said finally.

I followed Joan upstairs to the living room, and upon entering it, stopped dead in my tracks. It was like that moment when you know the LSD has finally kicked in. Like when Dorothy understands—at a cellular level—that she is no longer in Kansas. Every square inch of Joan Weaver's walls was covered with a museum's worth of framed paint-by-number images.

A kind of hysterical laugh caught in my throat. I bit my lip as my eyes began scanning the entire … oeuvre. There were paint-by-number puppies, clowns, bouquets of umbrellas, children ice-skating, goldfish tossing beach balls, children licking ice cream cones, portraits of white Jesus, Dalmatians riding on fire trucks, rabbits in mid-hop, a lawn-level depiction of a black cocker spaniel running with a croquet mallet in its mouth, deer chewing meadow grass, bulldogs playing poker, an old ship captain puffing on a pipe, and a cartoon bee with his arm swung around a daisy's stem, his legs crossed like Mr. Peanut's.

"My hobby," Joan explained. "I work in acrylic only. It relaxes me."

"You must be very relaxed," I joked. Joan glanced up at the ceiling as if my wisecrack had literally gone over her head. "Have you ever tried free-hand?" I asked, having no idea what to call paintings *without* numbers.

"I like paint-by-numbers," she explained, "because I always know how each picture will turn out."

"I see," I said. "Like reading the last page of a novel first. I do that."

Joan replied by staring blankly at her feet.

Where I came from, paint-by-number pictures were ironic, kitsch, something collectors find at tag sales and flea markets. I didn't even know you could still buy a paint-by-number kit.

I grew up with original artwork on the walls. We weren't wealthy, but art was something that was important to my folks. I inherited some of it and couldn't wait to hang it up in our new home.

From what I could gather, Joan's works were a form of art therapy. After my initial shock had subsided, I realized that I found her paintings moving. Thinking that instantly made me feel guilty, like I was looking down my nose at her for having created these pieces that were ... what? Facsimiles of real art? Were they any less real than the *Mona Lisa* or a painting that one of my children made? Who the hell was I to judge Joan Weaver and her paint-by-number acrylics? If her muse was manufactured in a factory or on an assembly line, so be it.

"Well, it's lovely," I said, hoping to sum up the art and the house all at once and get the hell out of there.

Joan's eyes settled on the carpet as she thanked me. "So, um, where did you move from?" she asked cautiously, presumably not wanting to pry.

"The city. We were downtown."

She looked at me directly for the first time. "I'm so sorry," she said. A moment passed in silence. "C'mon," she said brightly. "I want to show you my studio."

Joan led me downstairs to the den where an easel was set up in the corner next to a loveseat covered with stacks of neatly folded laundry. Leaning against it was a paint-by-number image of a fairytale cottage set in the middle of the woods.

"For you," she said, handing it to me. "Welcome to the neighborhood."

The picture was signed and framed under glass. I was flabbergasted. When I finally got back to the house, I made a fuss—I think the word is *flourish*—over the gift she had presented to me.

"Oh my," Dan said politely and with a smidgeon of apprehension in his voice.

Joan smiled lightly and folded her arms across her belly, each hand cupping the opposite arm's elbow. Lewis' eyebrows seemed to whirl like helicopter blades, an apparent sign of pride in his wife's artistic abilities and unparalleled flair for gifting.

"Well, we better be going," Lewis said as though a gong had sounded in his head, signaling time was up on this neighborly interaction. The Weavers said goodbye, promising future play dates and potluck dinners.

Dan had barely closed the front door and locked it when he asked, "Okay, what are we doing with the painting?"

The four of us settled into the kitchen.

"Put it in the garage?"

"What if the garage door is open and they see it?"

"The attic?" I suggested.

"What if they come over and don't see it hanging up?" our son asked sensibly.

"You think they would ask where it is?" I flicked my eyes at Dan for an answer.

"*He* might," Dan replied.

"Right," I said. "She's too polite to say anything, but I wouldn't want to hurt her feelings."

"Hm," my husband said, giving it some thought. "An albatross."

"What's that?" our daughter asked sleepily.

"Something you have to keep that you don't want," Dan explained.

"There's nothing hanging on the walls yet anyway," I said. "So for now, it makes no difference."

"*And* you said 'thank you,'" our son argued, shrewdly.

"True," I said. "And so what if they don't see the picture hanging up? Do we really care what our neighbors think?"

It was a question I never would have asked in New York City.

We all looked at Dan, our moral barometer, for the answer. He leaned his back against the fridge and folded his arms across his chest. "No," he said, finally. "We don't. We really don't care what the neighbors think."

I set out four bowls, milk, and a box of cereal. Dinner was served.

FUN

ELLIE DVORKIN DUNN

I am a 42-year-old big sister, sipping piña coladas at a restaurant on Ft. Lauderdale Beach with my 38-year-old little brother, with whom I have nothing in common but DNA. He shifts his gaze from the ocean to me, flashes a big doofy grin, and says, "This is fun, right?"

I half-heartedly smile and nod, mostly to appease him, but I am stressed as fuck. The whole reason we're in Florida is because our mother is in heart failure and we're waiting for her to get a cardiac catheterization, a test that will tell us whether she needs a stent or bypass surgery or some other procedure, and therefore nothing about this trip feels fun. Not leaving my husband and 5-year-old son in New York for an unknown amount of time, not spending bundles of money on airfare and hotels and gas, and certainly not this bathtub-sized glass of rum and fruit juice concentrate with an umbrella in it … though it *is* taking the edge off a teensy bit, I must say.

"Hey!" says my brother, like the lightbulb of the century has just gone off in his brain. "Wanna go with me to this 70s themed dance club tonight? It's gay, so no one will try to hit on you."

"Uhhhhh … no?" I say. "This isn't a vacation, Phil. We don't know how long we're going to be here so we should probably take it easy and get some sleep and not spend all our money on things like drinking and dancing."

"Fine," he says. "I'll take you back to the hotel, but I need to blow off some steam."

I hate him right now. He does whatever the hell he wants, while I have always been the responsible one, waking us both up for school and getting us dressed and pouring our cereal and packing our lunches. Dad always left for work early and Mom didn't feel the need to get out of bed, so there never seemed to be any other choice. However, our mother *would* rouse shortly before we walked out the door and call me into her room, so she could see what I was wearing for the day. It wasn't to give approval on my outfit, though; it was so she could provide an accurate description of me to the police in case I was kidnapped.

Mom not only saddled me with the morning routine, she also tasked me with putting my brother to bed at night, bribing me with the offer to stay up late and watch *Trapper John, MD* with her if I could get him to go to sleep. I even gave us both baths, which is how, when I was 8 and he was 4, I noticed my brother had a hernia which would require a surgical operation. Who knows how long it would have gone undiagnosed if I hadn't been taking such good care of the little asshole?

So I'm pissed at her for being such a crappy parent, and I resent having to be in Florida with Phil in the interest of *her* health and well-being. I take a long sip of my *colada* until it makes that loud slurping sound signaling I've reached the bottom of the bowl.

"Do you think she's gonna die?" Phil asks.

I'm pretty buzzed at this point, so I say, "I don't know. But sometimes I think it would be easier if she did."

I am an 8-year-old big sister about to go to Atlantic City with my 4-year-old little brother because that's what we do on most Saturdays in the summer.

My dad will be at work all day because he owns a pharmacy, so my mom always brings a babysitter with us so that she can spend most of her time at the casino. The sitters' names are always Marie or Maria, which I think has something to do with the Catholic school they all go to. Today, we're picking up Maria McGloughlin, who isn't as pretty as Maria Macreena, but she's much nicer than Marie Kavanaugh, so I'm really looking forward to it.

It's a long drive, so we play "I Spy" and "I'm Going on a Picnic," and when we get really noisy, my mom tells us to look out the window for pink bunny rabbits. I doubt they exist, but she assures us she has seen them, and Maria plays along and why would she lie? So we look. Just as I'm getting really annoyed that I haven't seen one, we park the car, hop out, and walk directly to the beach. My mom comes along, but as usual she isn't wearing a bathing suit. She kicks off her shoes and rolls up her pants and wades into the ocean with us for about five minutes before handing Maria some money and saying, "Meet me at the Tropicana around 5 o'clock." And she is gone.

Mom never packs any toys to build sandcastles, so we use our hands to push the sand into a giant mountain shape and decorate it with seashells and bottle caps. When that gets boring, we walk to the edge of the ocean and dig our toes in, and we scream when it seems like the water is going to pull our feet away. We hear the Jack & Jill man ringing his bell, and we beg Maria to buy us some ice cream from his freezer on wheels. She uses some of the dollars Mom gave her, and Maria and I both get mint chocolate chip, which is our favorite, and Phil gets boring vanilla. We try to lick it up before it melts all over our hands. I feel something land in my hair.

"Maria?" I say. "Was that my ice cream or was that a bird?"

She looks. "Bird. Finish your ice cream and we'll go in the ocean and rinse your head."

I hate crying in front of babysitters because I'm supposed to be a big girl, but I can't stop the tears. I finish my cone as fast as I can and wait for my brother to finish his so we can get the poop out of my hair. Maria does it very carefully because she knows I don't like getting my head soaked, and while she combs her fingers through my tangles, she sings a little of this really cool song I like: *They said it really loud, they said it on the air, on the radio. Whoa, oh, oh, on the radio.*

"All better now?" she says.

I nod, and we head to the Boardwalk.

We go into the first arcade we find and play Skee-Ball and Whack-A-Mole and Pac-Man. When we get tired of the games, we find a candy shop and buy saltwater taffy and hunks of chocolate fudge. We wash it all down with ice cold Cokes, and Maria lets out these long disgusting burps that make us laugh until my brother gets the hiccups. When my mother's wad of cash runs out, it is time to go find her at the casino.

We walk through the doors of the Tropicana and shiver because we are still wet, and the casino is freezing. It's very noisy because of all the jackpot bells and people cheering when they win, shouting curse words when they lose. There are lots of flashing lights and weird ugly colors on the carpet, but we stare down at it anyway so we don't have to look at the grownups with cigarettes waving, "Hi, Cutie" as we wander around, searching for my mom. A security guard stops us, telling us we are too young to be in here, and he walks us back to the front door to wait while they page my mother.

It's probably hard to hear an intercom announcement over all that casino noise when you're concentrating on poker or craps or whatever, so it takes a long time for her to come and find us. My brother's teeth chatter. Maria wraps a towel around him and tries not to look worried. This is taking forever, and I wonder if maybe Mom went to Caesar's Palace for better luck. I see her walking toward us.

Mom is always in a really good mood when she wins money, but today she must have lost because she sweeps past us saying, "Let's go!" We follow her outside, trying to hide our giggles every time she says, "Where the fuck did I park???"

We load into our car seats in the back and Maria sits up front. We hit traffic and it doesn't take long before my brother and I are fast asleep. When my mother wakes us up, we are home. I start to cry again because Maria has already been dropped off and I didn't get a chance to say good-bye, but my mother tells me to stop being such an actress. I don't really understand what that means, but I wipe my tears and go inside.

I am a 42-year-old big sister, crying in my 38-year-old little brother's rental car as we drive away from the hospital. We have just found out three things: 1. My mother gambled almost all her social security check in the first two days of the month, 2. She has less than a hundred and twenty dollars to last her the *rest* of the month, and 3. She doesn't need any kind of surgery, just an adjustment to her medication along with a change in diet and exercise. The word "change" is bitterly hilarious to me, because she is incapable of change.

After she admitted to me that she was out of money, she looked at me with pathetic eyes and said, "What am I going to do?" as if none of it was her fault. As if it had inexplicably happened *to* her. The rage seeped from deep in my stomach to high in my chest. I got up from the visitor's chair next to her hospital bed, leaned in really close to her face, and said, "I. Don't. Feel. Sorry for you."

I broke down because even after all she had subjected me to, spitting bile at her in her moment of vulnerability made me feel like a terrible person.

"I can see that you're upset," said my mother. "Why don't you just go?"

"No," I said. "I want you to watch me cry. I want you to see how sad I am."

No wonder I'm "such an actress." This is some dramatic shit.

When my brother walked in from getting coffee and learned what was going on, he got angrier than I have ever seen and said, "I wish you never got any of Dad's retirement money. You don't deserve a penny of it. You disgust me!" We walked out together and left her there alone.

Now we're in the car, and I'm crying, and my brother grips the steering wheel so tightly his knuckles have no blood in them. But instead of cursing or punching something, he says, "Let's go to that club."

My hair is frizzy from the Florida humidity. My makeup is smudged from all the tears, and I am not dressed for going out, but after two vodka tonics I don't care anymore. A giant image of Donna Summer appears on the video screen by the dance floor, and I hear it:

I never told a soul just how I've been feeling over you ... But they said it really loud, they said it on the air, On the radio. Whoa, oh, oh on the radio.

I follow my brother through the crowd, and we secure a spot right under a disco ball that was supposedly salvaged from Studio 54. We proceed to bust a move. It is an epic release to get swept up in the music and the strobe lights, to be part of the energy of a bunch of bodies moving all at once. I am not a terrible person. I am a daughter, dancing away a lifetime of parental damage. I am a mother, dancing like I'll never let myself do the same to my son. I am a big sister, dancing with my little brother, and we are a team who will tackle this together, despite our differences. I let myself close my eyes and feel the pulsating beat. When I open them again, I see Phil beaming at me.

"I told you this place was fun," he says.

Instead of launching back some snarky retort, I simply return his infectious smile and say, "Yeah. You were right."

COMING & GOING

September 30th, 2020
Virtual Show | Zoom

Podcast Episode 55

"The Faith of Candy"
written by Nancy Agabian
and performed by Charlotte Marchant

"Cookie"
written by Charlotte Marchant
and performed by Nancy Agabian

Tim Lindner | Producer and Story Coach

In 2020, *No, YOU Tell It!* reached its 9th year, the same year COVID-19 swept the world, taking with it too many lives and too much joy. The March show was shut down along with the rest of the world. Lockdown continued, forcing us to cancel the Lambda Literary team-up show planned for May. Come September, as our second scheduled Brooklyn Book Festival Bookend Event approached, we pivoted to combine shows with the May storytellers who agreed to swap tales virtually. "Coming and Going" was on!

The year before, I watched the Bookend Event story swaps at The Astoria Bookshop as an audience member. I dropped in, as I had for several prior *NYTI* shows, taking photos, laughing and crying with the rest of the audience. In the summer of 2020, I jumped in to help restart the series as a story coach and social media content creator.

There was so much for us to learn and relearn in this newly fractured world: how to spotlight in Zoom, how to do these stories justice through a computer screen, how to interact with people. On a weekday night that September, we joined the first story meeting one by one, showing up in little boxes, mostly strangers.

The connections we make when sharing stories is something writers can't fully express to their friends and families. You're so vulnerable. You're trusting others with your work! When we were living in isolation, seeing and hearing these unique tales for the first time, even virtually, it made us feel *human* again. And feeling human through this vulnerability wasn't the "new normal" we heard on the news; it was a return to the emotions and experiences we needed to get through life, to feel joy.

Charlotte Marchant and Nancy Agabian wrote from wildly different circumstances. Nancy's story portrays how, after relocating back to her suburban hometown prior to the pandemic to help her aging parents, COVID causes the lines between parent, child, and caretaker to blur. Charlotte's tale takes us on a journey back to her early days of protest and how her experience in jail shaped her sociopolitical identity. These stories felt both universal and personal to me with the rise of Black Lives Matter protests across the country while living at home with my parents throughout COVID. I could feel the frustration and anxiety when Nancy describes her father defiantly fighting for his car for an *unessential* outing. So many people broke with logic to cope with the pandemic as they knew how. I understood her helplessness as she suddenly became the protector of the most vulnerable.

Throughout the writing process, Charlotte recalled adding some literary elements, like the repetition of taps on the prison walls for secret communication, to make the story come to life. Which it did. Nancy shouting "POWER TO THE PEOPLE" at the end of the story was something that sent chills through the computer screens and down our spines. Nancy later described this commanding scream as a great relief.

I think the creative team felt relief and a coming-to-life too after we'd stumbled through some of the technical details and worried about if the online show would have the same impact. After being so far from everyone throughout 2020, these stories and performances reconnected everyone at that show, reminding us that we are still three-dimensional beings, with real experiences, memories, and feelings. At this moment it became clear that we all have stories and bringing them to life is more than just possible—it's necessary.

No, YOU Tell It! brings storytellers and curious people together, helping us learn about the unique experiences of individuals while feeling a deep connection to them. Our first virtual show was a success, and with it came new viewers from across the country, new technical knowledge, new interactions between the storytellers and audiences. I felt inspired, connected, and perhaps, for the first time in a while, a bit of joy. I hope these stories do the same for you.

THE FAITH OF CANDY

NANCY AGABIAN

"Nance, I need the keys to the car," my father calls outside my bedroom door.

I sigh, readying for a confrontation. It's early April 2020, and my ninety-year-old father, who is cognitively impaired, doesn't understand the new risks we face.

"What for?" I ask.

"I need to go to Walgreens to get snacks."

"Dad, you can't go—"

"WHY?" he bellows with such force that my heart jumps and my nerves jangle.

"Dad, it's dangerous for you to go out because of the virus."

Before I can tell him that Walgreens is Ground Zero of sick people, he pulls out his wallet and holds it up to me in the darkness of the hallway. From my bedroom window, sunlight shines on half of his angry face, his pointed nose and furrowed, bushy eyebrows. "I have a driver's license! It was renewed a couple of months ago!"

"It doesn't have to do with that," I explain. "There's an order for older people to stay at home because they will get very sick if they catch the virus."

I've explained this before, but the information isn't sticking. A month into the quarantine, I've been noticing that my parents' cognitive abilities are more limited. Their lives aren't so different from before, but even the lack of a few health care providers interacting with them during the day, and the loss of a few activities at the senior center during the week, must be making those neural pathways more narrow and rigid.

My father is on a rampage. I drop what I'm doing and find him in the living room, rummaging through my mother's pocketbook. Thankfully, I hid all the car keys a couple of weeks ago.

My mother doesn't seem bothered by my father's intrusion into her purse. "Mom, did you ask Dad to get you snacks?"

"I want cookies," she says innocently.

My mother started to lose her short-term memory four years ago. We were all surprised when my father followed suit a couple years later. Now my mother's personality has transformed to be more playful and childlike, complementing her shrinking stature and her wide brown eyes. I've gotten used to the role reversal.

"I'll get you a cookie," I reply.

As I open a kitchen cabinet to retrieve a sugar-free shortbread — my mother is on the verge of diabetes — I overhear my father asking why he can't have one. "Who made her the Ayatollah?" my American-born, Armenian dad asks. I find the randomness of his jab pretty funny, wondering how this unseemly reference to a villain from the 1970s hostage crisis surfaced from my father's memory banks. I stifle a smile.

After traveling every two weeks from New York to this Boston suburb for the past couple of years, I decided to move for a year to help transition my parents to receive more care. For a while I questioned my decision, giving up my apartment, my job, my writing, and any chance to date. When the pandemic arrived, it removed most of my doubt. Here was a good reason to be here.

Still, it would be nice to be appreciated as a caring daughter instead of likened to a Muslim fundamentalist dictator.

A few days later, I am reminded how stultifying it can be to have someone care for you. After three weeks alone with my parents, 24/7, I'm on edge and desperately need a walk. I can't get out the door without my mother interrogating me: Where am I going and for how long? Sometimes her fears drop from her mind along with her other short-term memories, and other times they burrow deeper. It's not uncommon for her to call me several times while I'm on a walk, warning me not to enter the park because it is desolate and unsafe. In reality, the park is populated with children at play, speed-walking moms, and retirees strolling with their dogs. For a while, I showed her photos of the park to prove the absence of roving bands of hoodlums and rapists. It didn't help, so I've learned to lie. To save my mother from distress, I tell her I'm walking around the neighborhood.

Geriatric workers have a name for this phenomenon: "A therapeutic fiblet." It makes deceiving your aged parents sound a lot nicer, especially when you dump them off at assisted living for eternity, claiming it'll just be a short stay while their home is redone. How I wish I had given myself permission to lie to my mother all the times in my life she expressed alarm. Riding my bike to the mall with friends at twelve, driving across country after graduating from college at 22, traveling to Turkey in search of ancestral villages at 30, getting a Fulbright to Armenia at 38. All were met with urgent lobbying efforts to prevent me from leaving, insistence that my decision-making was not just flawed but foolish. Even at a young age I knew her response had less to do with me and more with her fear that I would face harm. I argued vehemently, and she always somehow came around, but on her own terms, not without more warnings and a few I-told-you-so's. She had lost her mother to cancer when she was just nineteen, a trauma reverberating throughout her life. Did those arguments with me make her trauma bury deeper into her bones and muscles, hardening her brain tissue? Though I rationally know my mother has dementia, my body still can't help being triggered by her mania, automatically irritated, physically caught in a codependent boomerang.

When I arrive at the park, I disregard a new sign posted that it is closed due to COVID. For the past three weeks it has been packed with Millennials who have nowhere else to go outside their homes. Today I have the empty park all to myself and breathe in my oasis, filled with trees, light, and chirping birds.

On the way back home, however, my mother's looping fears rise in me when I see a lone man with a dog. He's tall and I get a funny feeling I shouldn't walk through the wooded part of the park. Lately I've been noticing that I assume the worst about the people who live here—that they're too stupid to follow safety precautions, that they will walk too close to me or cough in my direction. I remind myself there are bad people everywhere. I often encountered them in NYC where I lived for twenty years before relocating back to my suburban hometown. The fact that there are good people everywhere, too, comes to me at a delay as I head up our street. Has the stress of COVID—and the threat of it taking my parents away from me—exacerbated my fears? I feel like I've turned into my mother.

I'm about five houses from my parents' house when I notice a car coming around the turn. It is a deep purple, almost black. Maybe it's the light, but it appears to be my father's Scion. Before the numerals on the license plate can register, I see my father behind the wheel in his khaki jacket and baseball cap.

In an instant he is past me. I turn around and wave both arms like a deranged flight controller on the tarmac. He doesn't stop.

God damn it! My father has escaped quarantine!

The rest of the walk home is a blur. I try my best not to panic.

"Where's Dad?" I ask my mother, sitting in her living room chair.

"I think he went to that candy store on Route 1 that sells ice cream."

Only essential services are open, so Patwell's must be closed. I am not sure where my father could possibly go to retrieve whatever treat she has requested. Maybe to Big Y, our corner grocery store, or Walmart, just across from it on Route 1. It will be a disaster if he goes to either big box store crowded with throngs of germy people desperate for toilet paper. Rage overcomes me: heart racing, shallow breaths, tense spine.

"I have given up my life moving into this house to help you, and you keep fucking everything up with your constant requests for food!"

My mother doesn't yell back. Something sinks in. Perhaps the F word. I don't feel good about this outburst, but it seems significant, like tearing open a life-changing letter. I've admitted that I have moved here, which I have been eliding, mostly to protect myself from possible criticism, but also to shield my mother from possible shame for needing help. Months later, it will be clear the significance is only mine; my mother's brain won't retain that I've moved. Every day she will experience me as visiting from New York City.

I drive up to Big Y and the eggplant Scion is not in the parking lot. On the way to Walmart, I drive past home in case my father has returned. Lo and behold, he is in the driveway getting out of the car. When I pull up, he looks my way, sees me behind the wheel, and gives me a shit-eating smirk.

We manage to reach the front door at the same time.

"Where the fuck have you been?" I ask, wielding the f-word again as if it will help.

My father answers, "To Patwell's to get sugar free dark chocolate for your mother."

I am astonished Patwell's is open. How is candy essential? In a few moments I call them up, explain what just happened, and ask if they maintained distancing with my father. I get into an argument with the owner over their decision to not wear masks—it's a question currently being asked in the media if the public should wear them since it's been newly revealed that asymptomatic people can spread the disease. She said the public health department said masks were unnecessary for their protection. I tell her my father is 90 years old and has dementia and congestive heart failure. This is who they need to protect.

"Maybe *he* should wear a mask then," she replies.

At dinner, I am despondent. I've tried so hard to protect my parents, but I have failed. My body feels slammed, deflated, every fiber defeated. I eat my food silently.

Later that evening my father apologizes, and I do too.

"The reason I get upset about you going out is that if you are exposed to the virus, you will die," I tell my parents.

My mother's eyes widen. "No, we won't," she says, shaking her head, unaware of the crisis. In her pink bathrobe, with her fluffy white hair, she looks like an Easter Peep.

"Yes, Nancy's right," my father informs her soberly. "You don't have to worry about me," he says, handing me the car keys.

I'm relieved, but the next day I overhear my father on the phone telling my sister that I was upset when he went to Patwell's because I don't think he should drive. He has forgotten the virus again. The moment with his wallet and the driver's license comes back to me.

Driving has long been part of his identity. Before we had GPS, he was a human one, discovering and retaining innumerable routes and shortcuts on back streets, figuring out where landscapes lined up.

A few days later, we order Chinese food for pickup. I sit in the passenger seat and let my father drive, figuring it will be good for his self-worth after staying home for a few weeks. The trip to the Chinese restaurant is a regular route, but he forgets where to turn a couple of times, and I have to prompt him.

Perhaps my father conflated the virus with driving because he is actually scared that *he* shouldn't drive anymore.

Am I losing the ability to intuit these kinds of connections? During this life in quarantine, have my senses dulled, too?

A couple of weeks after my father's escape to the candy store, I bring out an old boom box and play CDs. One is titled *70 Years of Broadway*. We hear a singer crooning, "I think of you, night and day."

"Do you know who wrote this song?" my mother asks.

"No, but I can look it up." I assume she is asking to help her remember.

"Cole Porter," she says, her eyes dark and knowing.

For a minute my mother is back, the cultured, intelligent woman, the former teacher and cultural coordinator, not a little old white-haired urchin subject to her most base desires for sweets. My father also has some part of himself intact—his sense of duty as a provider, which compelled him to secure sugar-free chocolate for his prediabetic partner. Though the virus locks us down and upends our lives, it also exposes our truths.

I'm not sure if Patwell's ever shut down, but we will soon visit a few times for ice cream over the summer when it's safer. It's a really cute, family-run candy store that has been around forever. Walking inside is like opening a portal to happiness, with truffles in glass cases and bonbons displayed on red gingham tablecloths. Everything is made on the premises; there's even a glass booth where you can watch workers in aprons dip candy. It's one of my favorite places to visit around here actually. The staff are always kind and patient with my parents, too. If they hadn't been open, my father may have gone to Walmart or Big Y or even Walgreens, where he would have faced a much higher risk of exposure.

As hard as I try to shield my parents from COVID, I have to accept that there is only so much I can control. Where I can't reach, faith will have to fill in. Perhaps we're all dealing with some level of dementia as we don our masks and go about our day, plunging into the unknown, toggling fear, anger, grief, and faith in various doses. I imagine how it must have felt for my mother when she parented me as a child. Terrified of loss, yet confronted by a creature who simply needed to grow, she must have encountered faith on the flip side of her fear. Like day and night, night and day.

COOKIE

CHARLOTTE MARCHANT

My anger at America's involvement in the Vietnam War, along with my own need to belong to a community of kindred spirits, led to my joining the radical Weatherman organization and their Chicago "Days of Rage" demonstrations in October 1969. I was twenty years old, running frantically from cops on horseback as I threw rocks at the plate glass windows of corporate America, which just bounced right back at me. It was the men in Weatherman who went right up to those windows and swung heavy metal chains that brought the glass crashing and showering down onto the sidewalk. I was in Weather*man*, an organization whose name didn't even include me. My awareness of the feminist movement simmered on the back burner, not quite ready to come to a boil. When the cops first grabbed me, I felt terrified along with some relief. It was over. I had been caught and arrested for rioting along with others in Weatherman. I could stop running and at last get some rest. Being a revolutionary was exhausting.

Standing tall before the judge, stretching to be all five-foot-one inch of myself, I said what I had memorized earlier with as strong a voice as I could summon: "Your honor, I'm not guilty. The US government is guilty of killing innocent Vietnamese people and using poor and Third World Americans as cannon fodder." He decided otherwise, pronounced me guilty, and sentenced me to thirty days in Chicago's Cook County Jail.

Arriving at the jail, I heard the echoes of jail life. I heard male inmates shouting messages from one cell to another. "Hey, Carlos, man! Your boy Tito was brought in last night. They gave him 60 days for possession, man. He's strung out real bad. Hangin' over the fuckin' toilet throwin' up all night. Got the shakes today. He's real fucked up."

At the women's section on the jail's top floor, I was handed a scratchy gray blanket, a tin plate, a spoon, and a stiff yellow, faded dress uniform. The guard took me to my seven-by-eight-foot cell containing a metal bed, sink, and toilet. I sat on my bed trying to take in what would be my new reality for thirty days. I was thankful my time had an end date, aware that wasn't the same for others. Any fear I had about being in jail slowly dissipated when I entered the dayroom where we were cheered by the women inmates gathered there. They had been watching the demonstrations on the news and were very curious to learn more about "the crazy white people rioting in the streets."

It was in the dayroom shared by the women inmates that I first heard the knocks on the sheet metal walls, *Boom-Slap-Boom*, from the male inmates on the floors below. It was a form of inter-jail communication the inmates had created to maintain some sense of control over their lives. Sometimes the knock was made with force using the side of a fist — *Boom* — or with an open hand — *Slap* — or with knuckles making a *Tap*. Like playing a conga drum, different beats were created — *Tap-Slap-Tap-Boom* — in different rhythmic patterns — *Boom-Tap-Slap-Tap* — and assigned as a phone number and memorized. If the woman who was being called wasn't around, the other women shouted through the cell block to let her know "her man" was on the "phone." She returned her knock pattern and went to the cells to answer the call. Everyone knew each other's phone numbers.

When a woman was called, she went to the prearranged cell that was above the one her male caller was in — one to three floors below. Lying down some blankets on the hard, cold, concrete floor, she got comfortable and spoke into the sides of the vents where the sheet metal walls met at an angle and there was just enough space to feel a small draft. These phone calls sometimes went on for hours. Some callers were just friends; others became "lovers." Many of the women had more than one "lover" and used aliases with different personalities depending on who was calling. They put one guy on hold and ran to another cell to talk with someone else.

One night, Rita, an inmate whose thick brown arms were scarred from years of drug use, had arranged with a sympathetic guard to be locked in a cell with the clearest sounding vents. It was going to be a big night for Rita and her "lover" Raymond. She had gotten a glimpse of his fine and muscular body through the dayroom window when she saw him below emptying trash in the yard. *Boom Boom Slap*—she called him for their date. My cell was directly across from the one Rita had chosen for the night. After the guard made her evening rounds, Rita carefully set up her blanket and pillow on the cold floor. Soundproofing being what it was, we all heard everything without even trying. Rita stretched out on the blanket and put her ear to the cold metal. Soon Raymond's voice traveled up the three floors and her body was warm again. Rita told him how much she loved him and began to describe the pleasures she would give him, if only she could. She placed her hand between her legs and did for herself what we could all only imagine Raymond said he would have done. Her passionate moaning filled the jail cells. Rita was making love for all of us.

I lay on my bed under the scratchy gray blanket watching through the bars as snow flurries fell. I listened to Rita and could only imagine what Raymond was saying and doing. During their ritual I was like an eavesdropper invading her privacy and eventually I felt turned on.

Rita had several different phone callers. Some were just friends, and others became lovers. Her friend Cookie, who she used to run numbers with in Chicago, told her he wanted to meet one of the women in Weatherman. Those of us remaining in jail met, and I was chosen to be the contact. I was a little nervous the night of our first call. Since it seemed that most of the "relationships" over the vents were sexual, I was afraid of Cookie's expectations of me. My growing awareness of my own sexuality had just started emerging that year. I still felt shy enough about the sounds, smells, and tastes of it all in private to even imagine having a public showing like Rita's the night before. My sexual interest and experience with women was just getting started. The sexual freedom encouraged in the Weatherman collectives allowed me to explore my bisexuality. It was a year later that I cut my long dark hair short, declaring myself a Lesbian. In the midst of all these sexual awakenings, I planned to keep my "relationship" with Cookie on a purely cerebral level.

Our knock was *Tap-Tap Boom Tap*. He rang, I returned the knock and went to my cell. Cookie reassured me that he wanted to only have political dialogue. When I replied, "Right on," he was delighted and asked me to say it again. He said, "Never heard a white girl talk that way before." He was in jail for armed robbery, awaiting trial, and facing up to ten years. He liked the Black Panthers and was against the war in Vietnam. Cookie wanted to talk every evening after the news and discuss what we had heard. Whenever I'd say, "Right on" or "Power to the People," which I said a lot in those days, he laughed with pleasure and asked me to say it again. Sometimes he called just to hear me say it. I was relieved to keep the conversation on this level, avoiding any possibility of sexual talk.

One night I heard his *Tap-Tap Boom Tap* call and didn't answer because I was too busy discussing political theory from Chairman Mao's Little Red Book with my comrades. *Tap-Tap Boom Tap*, he continued knocking for me most of the evening. *Tap-Tap Boom Tap Tap-Tap Boom Tap*. He eventually called Rita, who relayed the message that Cookie was pissed off and wanted me to return his calls. When I did call him back, he yelled in a stern voice, "*You* have to answer when *I* call, and who do *you* think you *are* anyway?" Well, I told him a thing or two about my priorities, "*I* don't have to come when *anybody* calls me unless it's a person in uniform, and what's *Power to the People* all about anyway?" He eventually calmed down and said I was right; it was just that he looked forward to our daily talks and was disappointed when I wasn't there. We resumed our nightly discussions with the understanding that I wasn't always available to answer his calls.

We argued about the right time to make Revolution in this country. He thought it was years away, if at all, while I was positive it was only a matter of months. As the last days of my sentence were drawing near, Cookie got news from his lawyer that he might be released sooner. His conversation turned to everything he'd do when he got out. "I know the perfect restaurant to take you to—soft music, candlelight, and wine." I told Cookie, "Hold on there. It sounds like you have expectations that we already talked about not having." He told me, "I couldn't help it; I've fallen in love with you. I'm in love with your mind. I never even asked you what you looked like and don't even want to know." He almost got me there until I remembered Rita probably shared my description with him. He said he loved my thoughts and ideas. "I want us to be together so I can hear you say, 'Right on' and 'Power to the People' for the rest of my life."

I told him I wasn't planning to spend time going to candlelit restaurants, that my life was dedicated to the Revolution. He was glad I wanted to change the world, but he was convinced that when we met at that restaurant he'd turn my head around, and I'd relax a little and see things his way. The night before my release I lay in my cell thinking about saying goodbye to Cookie. I was already missing our evening news analysis and the bobbing and weaving I had to do to avoid the sexual innuendo, which seemingly came out of nowhere. In the middle of talking about the pros and cons of non-violence, Cookie said things like: "I bet you like taking hot baths with scented candles all around!" And he was right, I did. On that last morning, I knocked — *Tap-Tap Boom Tap* — and sadly said, "Right on" and "Power to the People" to Cookie through the vents for the last time.

Years later, when it was apparent the Revolution was not right around the corner, I ran into a male friend who had been in Cook County Jail. I asked if he had met Cookie there. He said everyone knew and respected Cookie. He heard he had been sentenced to ten years. Timidly, I asked him what Cookie looked like. He told me Cookie was a man who had been around. I had already known about the scar across his cheek from the knife fight in his teenage years. But I hadn't known that Cookie was well over seventy-years-old!

Now I could begin to understand why Cookie had a vision of the future that included so much more patience than mine. All the time we had spent talking through the vents, along with the bravado and sexual innuendo, he had tried to teach me that my dreams for revolutionary change took lots of work and especially time. A lesson, now that I am in my seventies, I thought I could finally hear.

However, the sounds of the young people taking to the streets shouting "Black Lives Matter" are calling to me. Maybe there's no time to waste and the Revolution is now. But where do I fit in? I once belonged to a band of novice warriors, and now the only "Tiger" in me is the brand name on my sneakers. On these marches, even those sneakers can't carry my tired legs across the bridges to Manhattan and back to Brooklyn. This pandemic has taken its toll on my body and my spirit, and sometimes I am a weary, worried warrior afraid of the virus, feeling replaced by the youth, without time on my side. I watch from afar, listening to their righteous chants and I shout to them in as strong a voice as I can summon: "Right on!" and "Power to the People!"

PRECIOUS

~~March 12th, 2020~~
December 10th, 2020
Virtual Show | Zoom

Podcast Episode 56

"Survey Says!"
written by Heather Quinlan
and performed by Sokunthary Svay

"I Heard Some Chords"
written by Sokunthary Svay
and performed by Heather Quinlan

Kelly Jean Fitzsimmons | Series Creator and Producer
&
Amanda Sisk | Alum Storyteller and "Precious" Director

On March 10th, 2020 we held "Precious" rehearsals. On March 11th, I made the tough call to "postpone" our live show scheduled for March 12th. The time between that canceled show to when we came back together, virtually, nine months later felt both fleeting and infinite.

I built the series from scratch in 2012. However, when COVID hit, followed by a family emergency that resulted in me going to live with my parents in Florida for almost a year, it was the *No, YOU Tell It!* community who supported me, helping me pivot to producing online shows.

Alumni storytellers Noah Diamond and Amanda Sisk, the dynamic duo who'd recently produced *Quarantigone* (a hilarious Zoom adaption of the Greek tragedy *Antigone*) added their talents to the *NYTI* online team. We worked together with Tim Lindner to give these virtual performances theatrical flair.

I wanted to revisit "Precious" to give the storytellers a chance to swap stories finally. I wanted to give back to the *NYTI* community by using part of our Queens Council on the Arts grant to purchase copies of storyteller Heather Quinlan's book *Plagues, Pandemics and Viruses: From the Plague of Athens to Covid-19* from our friends at The Astoria Bookshop. Plus, what bizarrely better prize could there be for our story trivia winners? Heather's book, which she'd started writing pre-pandemic, came out in the interim and included an interview with Dr. Fauci.

I didn't want to go back and revisit those March 10th rehearsals, the last day I'd been in Manhattan before the world fell apart. Embracing her newfound role, Amanda Sisk stepped up to direct all four "Precious" stories. Keeping in the spirit of our two-part show, I asked Amanda to describe her experience going from *No, YOU Tell It!* storyteller to Zoom director.

I'm sitting in a tiny room around a tiny table with six strangers, and we're talking about addiction, my father's death, and a night that almost destroyed my marriage. And I'm not even in an A.A. meeting. It's 2015; my first workshop as a *No, YOU Tell It!* storyteller. Story coaches and directors shuffle through and mark up the papers where I've laid out my darkest fears and craziest adventures. And, for some reason, I'm absolutely okay with it.

You learn to trust your *NYTI* team very quickly. Not just because you're intimately digging through each other's lives, but because it is evident from that first story meeting that these people are going to make your story better, make you think where you hadn't thought before … make you finish the damned thing.

Even on the big day, when you're sitting on stage, and someone is about to tell yet another group of strangers ALL about you, you don't feel separated. Your directors are looking at you encouragingly; your story partner stands next to you and delivers your piece with so much authenticity and context that you don't even remember where you started. You just know that it's "right" now. Your fellow writers hearing the final draft for the first time are engaged and expectant. They know where you started and where you've been. You are never alone.

So how does, say, a random director, nine months after an *NYTI* performance was scrapped because of the pandemic, tell four writers, "Hi, you don't know me and I know you worked on this already and you were originally directed by someone else and I don't really have any context, but I'll be taking over now. So, you know, remember everything you learned and forget everything you know and trust me."

208

I felt like an imposter, like I was on a tightrope—lean too far one way and lose the story; lean too far another way and lose the writer. My intention was to reshape what had already been created. I didn't want to cross boundaries. I didn't expect to add anything new. I admit, I fearfully held my breath and waited for the inevitable pushback.

Stepping in as their new *NYTI* team member, I found myself (virtually) face-to-face with an amazing group of writers who, for some reason, were absolutely okay with it. They welcomed me, opened themselves up to me, spent time with me, and generously gave me an opportunity to work with them and their inspired, inspiring, and hilarious tales.

No, YOU Tell It! creates little families through commonalities, whether it's how two of you approach a writing assignment the same way or that every single person's mother made them a totally embarrassing Halloween costume at some point in adolescence. The theme of the night holds the stories together. The writers, story coaches, and directors hold each other together in a circle of trust. That circle is where the art comes from; it's by sharing that the art is realized.

Life got hard in 2020. Everything changed, but we adapt. We disregard expectations. We plan, and God laughs. If I've learned one thing from directing, it's that nothing—not even a pandemic—can stop a determined artist. And thank the universe for that.

SURVEY SAYS!

HEATHER QUINLAN

When I found out I was going to be part of *No, YOU Tell It!* I was thrilled. When I found out the topic was precious, I was un-thrilled. Anything worthy of being called "precious" was too precious to me. My love for my fiancé? Daffodils by the side of the road? A childhood combing the weeds of Staten Island looking for dead bodies and occasionally finding one? Yeah, kinda. But that was more fun than precious. Christ—*precious*. I'm cringing.

It always seemed like the first meeting of *NYTI* was a week away, and as a procrastinator I was happy about that. I hadn't read Kelly Jean's email closely. I'd written down the date but figured we'd come in, introduce ourselves, talk about our pain, write down words, go home. Then I would have ANOTHER week after that to actually produce something. Whew! Back to napping.

When I told my plans to my fiancé, Adam, he told me, "I might be wrong, but I think you have to show up with a rough draft." Oh, God. I went back and re-read the email. Not only was he right, but I needed a first draft in two days and the suggested length was 1,600-1,700 words. I couldn't take a nap, and I would have to write many, many, many, many words.

During lunch in the kitchen with our friend Art, I tried to learn what they thought was precious. Art said, "gem" but he was eating a taco, so I thought it was "Jeff." Adam tried to get me brainstorming with, "Name five things…" which made me cut him off and say, "We asked 100 people, the top five answers are on the board, here's the question: 'Name something that's precious.'" This was *Family Feud*—in my mind the Richard Dawson one where he kissed all the lady contestants until Rock Hudson got AIDS. That show was a huge part of my childhood, pretty much anyone's childhood who grew up in the 70s and 80s.

As my uncle once said, "We all had the same six channels, we all watched the same shit."

So, I'm Richard Dawson, barely hiding my British accent, kissing all the birds, wearing a Botany 500 suit. Wait, no, I'm a contestant on

Family Feud with a Dorothy Hamill haircut getting kissed by Richard Dawson wearing a fake Halston. Me in the Halston, not him.

Again: "We asked 100 people, the top five answers are on the board. Here's the question: 'Name something that's precious.'" I have to hit the buzzer before my opponent who looks like he graduated from Cornell just to be on *Family Feud*. I don't have an answer, but I hit it anyway.

Me: _____

I am mute. The audience laughs.

Richard Dawson says, "Show me nothing!"

XXX!

Richard Dawson tells me that if it were up to him, Beefeater would be the #1 answer. Like I said, he's British.

He turns to my opponent who says, "gem" like Art did, and it's the #1 answer. Their team decides to pass. I go back to my family. There's no one there. The dream sequence dies.

I have a hard time saying what's precious because to give it a name would be to make it valuable and, therefore, dangerous.

I'll explain: My dad died in 1996, 24 years to the day after his brother Danny Boy died in a drunk driving crash. I quit drinking 19 years to the day after my dad died, 54 years after Danny Boy died.

Danny Boy was driving home from a party and was elected the least drunk. He drove Tommy Gorman's car straight into a tree. Danny flew through the window, the other guys got broken legs. My family was destroyed. I was 12 years from being born.

Also—also! Two years after that my grandfather's brother died driving drunk on Hylan Boulevard, coming home from a Christmas party. He hit a pole. Five years after that my grandmother's brother died while driving drunk and he hit a pole too.

Again: "We asked 100 people. The top five answers are on the board. Here's the question: 'Name something you drink to calm your nerves.'" I have to hit the buzzer before my opponent who looks like he graduated from Brown just to be on *Family Feud*.

Me: Nail polish remover!

The audience is silent.

Jolly Richard Dawson looks horrified, then turns and says, "Show me nail polish remover?"

XXX!

He turns to my opponent who stares open-mouthed for a moment, then says, "Beefeater" like Richard Dawson did and it's the #1 answer. Their team decides to pass. I go back to my family. There's no one there. The dream sequence dies.

I'm left alone on the floor of Family *Feud*. Cripes, I mean, even Richard Dawson's dead, so is Ray Combs who replaced him (hanged himself).

What my family valued, what we saw as precious, was what killed most of us. It was death and the inability to feel anymore. One person dies, the grief is unbearable, so the next person dies, and so on. More pain. A lovely death. That's it.

All the alcoholics in my family, except possibly for my Aunt Katie who I recently learned drank a bottle of Bailey's Irish Cream every day yet still weighed 100 pounds, were men. I was the one lady alcoholic. I didn't drink like a lady though; I didn't even drink like a human. Anything was fair game, starting with boxed wine and then Georgi Vodka. I decided if I didn't drink beverages it didn't count, so there was perfume, vanilla extract, almond extract (spicy!), nail polish remover … just not rubbing alcohol because Kitty Dukakis drank that and, when I heard about that as a kid, it terrified me. Alcoholics drink rubbing alcohol. Non-alcoholics drink nail polish remover.

The day I relapsed it was on rubbing alcohol. It's when I tried to die. I'm still here. What can I say? I'm inept.

It was the anniversary of all those deaths, and I just wanted to join them. I didn't even know Danny Boy, but I wanted to meet him. And I missed my father so much—just as much as if we'd buried him the day before.

Yet here I am. And I'm happy about it! If I'd died, it would've undoubtedly killed my mother, and that alone would be enough to send me to Hell. I never would've met Adam (at a party where we played a home-grown version of *Family Feud*), fallen in love, had the guts to propose to him, and start a new life. I never would've met my family in Ireland, who I connected with through a genealogy site, and they are the most wonderful people in the world! I'm a Quinlan, they're Quinlans—found my Quinlans! I was the lone Quinlan left barely standing till I found them in Tipperary, which my cousin Laura called "the Eltingville of Ireland." (Those of you from Staten Island will get it.) But I don't care. I regained a family to huddle with on *Family Feud*.

I hang out in cemeteries. Filming them, the art, the history, wondering about who's there, wondering if they know each other, like in "Our Town." I've often wondered if my dad is now friends with the people he's buried next to. I wrote their names down and thought about contacting their families but decided that was too weird. Still, you never know…

You could say I'm obsessed with death—from a distance. I'm writing a screenplay called "DIE BITCH DIE" about my stepmother (though in all honesty my cousin Dorothy came up with the title). I don't fear death—I need a mammogram. Breast cancer runs in my family—hell, all kinds of cancers do alongside alcoholism; we're really blessed. But I'm 45 and haven't gotten one yet. I'm not worried about dying. I'm not longing to die, but I am quite interested in it. Yet it's no longer precious to me.

I HEARD SOME CHORDS

SOKUNTHARY SVAY

Axl Rose was a damn banshee. My pre-pubescent self was struck by something in him that was unidentifiable to me at the time. He had a way with his snake-like side-to-side gyrating, the long red hair and bandana, songwriting, and melodies that remained in your mind's ear. Songs like "November Rain" and "Sweet Child O' Mine" remain in the cultural memory of Americana even as the times change.

I first heard Guns N' Roses in the Bronx at Alain's house, the friend of my older brother Thy. Actually, we, my younger brother Jammy and I, heard the music and the impression it left remains imprinted even now in my memories of growing up in the borough one normally associates with hip hop. The song? "Rocket Queen" from the *Appetite for Destruction* album. Alain, whom I had a 10-year-old crush on, asked if I wanted to try playing the bass. Duh! Then he taught me the two notes required to play during the second half of the song, where "Rocket Queen" took a completely different musical turn. My fingers were small, they always have been, but could pluck the strings. Connected to the amplifier, I heard my success throughout the entire room. I was hooked and so was Jammy. We wanted to hear more.

But our older brother Thy couldn't stand Axl Rose's (Guns N' Roses' lead singer) voice. This was a bit of an obstacle to our gathering of extremely limited funds. At that point, the music we were subjected to was under the tyranny of our older brother. (We spent a good few weeks listening to Irene Cara's *What a Feelin'* album every night before going to sleep.) He was more partial to freestyle, new wave, and some R&B; I leaned toward anything with a melody I could remember. No, there had to be another way that went around him.

We tried the New York Public Library's Morris Park branch in the northeastern part of the Bronx. I got my hands on the cassette tapes for *Use Your Illusions 1* and 2, a bit stimulated by some of the inappropriate imagery there on the latter, some illustrated boobs and panties down around a blonde woman's ankles. When I went to the library check out, barely tall enough to hand my library card to the seated employee, I was told I was too young to take it out and would require an adult. The plan was foiled! But the desire was implanted, and the roots of our love for guitar-based music were sewn.

Eventually, the grunge age ushered in, and we became obsessed with the idea of getting a guitar. *Wayne's World* had just come out and we wanted a guitar as badly as Wayne wanted the white fender Stratocaster, his dream guitar, in his local music shop where no playing of Led Zeppelin's "Stairway to Heaven" was allowed. Well, there *was* a guitar being sold at the lone independently owned music shop in Pelham Parkway where we bought all our cassette singles. It was around $130. Given that we had no allowance, never/could not/would not ask for money, $130 seemed insurmountable. It would take a little more than searching couch cushions for change to reach that kind of goal. Thy definitely wouldn't have supported such a habit. We had to live with the burn of that desire for a while.

Since it seemed impossible to get a guitar, we settled for just buying cassette tapes of bands whose singles we enjoyed hearing on the radio. Here's the thing, trying to get our hands on music was an expensive, time-consuming act. Borrowed music collections meant working with what was already there, pretty much settling, although sometimes you wound up with auditory gold. There were often advertisements for music memberships, like Columbia House, where to start you could get 10 albums (or so) for one cent, which dragged you into some membership you ultimately didn't want.

We often perused all the albums we dreamed of owning in those magazine adverts. Until I managed to find a kid who played saxophone in my symphonic band on Saturdays who had already gone through the trouble of taping one cent to the catalogue and putting it in the mailbox to redeem his desired music. That's when we broke Khmer kids who had suddenly moved to the projects, got our hands on Soundgarden, Pearl Jam, Smashing Pumpkins, Live, Stone Temple Pilots, and whoever's music tastes we were, again, at the mercy of.

By this point we were in the early double-digit ages, junior high and high school age, a highly un-coveted time in our childhood. This was also around the time that Gregorian chant album came out for which Tower Records had huge posters. It was there at the Lincoln Center Tower Records that I would listen to music samples at listening stations with enormous headphones and newly released albums, though rarely having money to buy anything. This meant going hungry if friends asked me to hang out, too ashamed to tell them why. It meant saving my lunch money and starving the whole day so I could afford Chinese buns instead while hanging in Chinatown with my friends. It meant I couldn't afford to pay for outings—let alone music—and more importantly, even if I could, I likely wouldn't be allowed to go because my parents wanted me home to the Bronx before it got dark.

My mother gave me an allowance of $3 a day while I was going to a specialized music and arts high school in Manhattan. I would play flute in chamber ensembles, symphonic bands (and eventually orchestra) during the day, but my heart was more into singing and the bands Jammy and I followed. I can't stress enough how not having access to money in a music economy that still depended on cassette and CD meant we were shut out from being able to purchase any kind of music whatsoever. This meant no Napster, no Spotify, no Amazon, no YouTube. It meant that if you liked music, you had to listen to the radio with a built-in cassette recorder and hoped your favorite song came on so you could press the record and play button at the same time to catch it—but only after the deejay would stop talking, because nobody wanted to record his voice. Cassette singles were a few bucks but limited you to one song, its remixes and a B-side that was a toss-up in terms of likability. For kids with parents living on a string, to buy any music was a precious thing. You would look for sales, tapes/CDs to borrow, watch *Saturday Night Live* if your favorite band performed, or wait for them to appear as guests on any other shows. Or if you happened to get a (blessed) subscription for cable, you could watch it on MTV or VH1.

At a certain point, however, we finally managed to purchase cassette tapes, and eventually some CDs of things we liked. However, the next issue was transporting the music. Sure, we could play CDs in the car but only Walkmans (portable cassette players) existed for commuting. (And don't even get me started on Discmans, which were portable compact disc players that were rendered useless if they weren't held upright!) My daughter's generation will never know the obsession of recording a song over and over again just to avoid rewinding a tape. (Song on loop, anyone?)

Since we were at an age where we still went on excursions with our dad, we decided to try out our "mixtapes" in his car. Jammy was proud of our 90s model Toyota Cressida and looked for any opportunity to play his/our music in the car. We knew our parents frowned on rap, such as Biggie Smalls, yet we managed to play "clean" versions of tracks with cussing dubbed out or playing hip hop instrumentals. We also played Guns N' Roses, too, and my mom thought the song title was "Welcome to the Junkie." We thought we were fucking cool.

I look back and think about what was even more precious than getting our hands on the music was the connection my brother and I solidified with this common want. We so badly wanted a guitar that we would hang out in my room, the lights dimmed, put on some rock, and use my extended desk lamp as a guitar.

The spring at the end was quite thick and we would pluck it (making very strange bass-like fuzzy twangs) to Stone Temple Pilots. It was better than air guitar. And we had good rhythm.

Speaking of which, my father never sung or danced in front of me my entire life. He also refrained from expressing emotion, aside from anger. I didn't know if it was because of his personality or because my parents had survived a genocidal Communist regime known as the Khmer Rouge in the late 70s; it's difficult to distinguish between who he was and what he'd been through, so I was left picking up clues to understand him. But goddamn he could tap out a rhythm in the car on the steering wheel. It was my way of knowing he was there listening to the same music as us, not lost in some reverie (which was how I always imagined him). We could always tell if he liked the music (or didn't hate it) by whether or not he would tap rhythmically to the song. We found that our dad's fingers seemed to like Guns N' Roses. Not a singer, Daddy's preferred sound was a grunt. Grunt of approval here, grunt of discontent there. It was the only unspoken word I registered from him that even resembled a melodic (this was pushing it), phonated utterance. (I'm taking some liberties here in my description because, after all, I'm the same person who played a desk lamp and heard a guitar.)

With the beauty and new eyes that adult hindsight allows, I look back at Axl Rose as more of a sex symbol, partly because of the confidence and looks he exhibited at the time, but more importantly I loved his audacity to move his body as he wanted, on stage no less! And the power to sing in a register that seemed unreal to me at the time, a range normally associated with women. I loved the convention-breaking. I wanted to sing like that. I wanted that freedom from the expectations imposed on my own body. We barely expressed emotions in our household. Words were practical, used sparingly aside from enforcing my parents' cultural expectations. In this house, I wanted to scream for all the times my body hurt, that my heart was pained. I couldn't even cry except in secret, to my ceiling at night. If I cried in front of my family, what would they do?

I never did. My biggest fear was they would say or do nothing. American TV set me up for lots of disappointment. I was bombarded by images of white parents giving affection to their kids, saying words like "love" and even asking how they were doing (a novel idea in a culture where asking if someone has eaten is our greeting). I loved singing in a large group but feared singing solos. What if my voice wasn't strong enough on its own? What if my voice faltered and couldn't hold the note? What if it wavered? What if I sounded weak? I still have dreams where I try to defend myself against some conflict, I find that I'm mute, and scream in silence despite my best efforts.

That lack of voice haunted me until I couldn't escape it. I became a mother and was diagnosed with postpartum depression in my early 30s. All those years of unheard words and unsung songs in our home finally caught up with me. I sought help with a therapist, worked on my mental wiring with some medication. It wasn't enough to sing songs, mere aesthetics of other people's words and sentiment. I had to know what I wanted to say as well as sing. The voice and song became one in me. As I reflected in the years following, I learned more about my vulnerabilities, the need to be seen and heard. As I rebuilt the melody of my life, singing became an easier effort, certainly with the help of my vocal teacher. And while I never did become a rock star like my tween self thought, I did just complete my first opera. I now write words so that other people can create melodies through them.

These days I sing a mean karaoke. "Paradise City" and "Welcome to the Jungle" are some of my favorites. It doesn't feel as naked to sing Axl's part since his upper range is comfortable for me; it doesn't require the amount of effort it takes him in that register. Who knew? Jammy has purchased a couple of guitars for himself, and the last time I saw him during vacation, I could hear him strumming guitar chords of some 90s tune, as though our interests hadn't changed at all in the last thirty years.

Without any personal instruction, he managed to learn to play some songs. Our younger selves would be so proud. Music was our way of creating a path for expression, something somatic and innate, partly because we hadn't been shown the words to express ourselves in the more essential everyday ways. For the times that spoken words weren't possible or enough, we let the vibrations of chords help us transcend those limitations.

WHAT I KNOW

March 7th, 2022
Culture Lab, LIC | Queens

Podcast Episode 63

"Knowing Is Half the Battle"
written by Sheria Mattis
and performed by Michele Carlo

"Viva La Curl-Volution!"
written by Michele Carlo
and performed by Sheria Mattis

Erika Iverson | Director and Founding Member

Born in the early 1970s, I suffered through decades of the same brown and orange décor shared by most kids of my generation. My mom was a big fan of a certain shade of orange best described as "damp rust."

As far back as I can remember, prominently displayed near the dryer and the sewing machine in my childhood home, there was a poster that perfectly matched the orange carpet in our basement. *"Marzo 8, Dia Internacional de la Mujer,"* it proclaimed, with strong graphic faces printed in brown, orange, and yellow—a reprint of a Cuban poster representing the women of the world.

Our "What I Know" show fell on the eve of March 8, International Women's Day in 2022. Back in front of a live audience and livestreamed to an even larger one, the night featured four writers pondering what it meant to identify as a woman, discussing issues of health, body image, feminism, colorism, and ageism. One non-binary writer wondered whether the title "woman" ever really fit them at all.

I'm always excited to rehearse with a *NYTI* storyteller one-on-one, and I love that after ten years, I almost always hear the same thing at that first read-through: "I really want to do my partner's story justice." We usually have just over an hour to work together, but I never have to worry the performer hasn't thought about their partner's story in advance.

After working for weeks as a group, each storyteller knows this real-life story has been carefully crafted. They've seen their story partner agonize over structure and phrasing, just as they've puzzled through changes to their own stories. The storyteller I'm assigned to work with will walk into the rehearsal room with a new realization and a strong conviction: My mission now is to do my very best to share my partner's story with our audience. In fact, you can hear Sheria Mattis express this in the show recording.

"Let me not cry," she says to story partner Michele Carlo, pausing to wipe her eyes before she begins, "You read the shit out of my story, let me do you justice."

I was thrilled to direct Sheria and Michele's story swap, although they didn't really need much help from me. Both came to us with extensive performance backgrounds, Michele as a storyteller and Sheria as a stand-up comedian. Both had killer stories with an unusual combination of humor and pathos. In our brief rehearsals, I had the pleasure of witnessing two brilliant performers at the height of their abilities sharing the deeply personal story of someone they had met just a few weeks before. Being a *No, YOU Tell It!* storyteller means our performers have to "walk in each other's shoes." In this case, two women of color from two different generations of New York City life traded tales with an intimate understanding of each other's experience.

Directing these stories made me think about mother-daughter relationships and what it means to be a woman, with all the complicated beauty and body issues that entails. What do we inherit from our mothers and what do we leave behind? How do things out of our control—fibroids, the color and texture of our hair—change our identity? And how far are we willing to go to wrest that control back into our own hands?

Working with *No, YOU Tell It!* challenges me to see things from new points of view, and hopefully lets others do the same. Since my mother's death, I've thought hard about continuing to expand the feminism I inherited from her to include a broader spectrum of sex, gender, race, and culture.

That International Women's Day poster now hangs on my wall in Brooklyn. Like Michele's hair and Sheria's fibroids, I've inherited it, and the questions that go with it, directly from my mother. Roughly 50 years after the printing of that poster, I'm still working on becoming a more inclusive feminist, writer, director, human. And like Michele with her hair, I've even come to appreciate that particular shade of orange.

KNOWING IS HALF THE BATTLE

SHERIA MATTIS

I used to think I knew my body, especially my pussy and all its accouterments. I took some health classes, I know about the clitoris, the cervix, and all the turkey giblets inside. But while I was walking around feeling cocky about my pussy, they were in there. Just sitting in my uterus. Listening. Plotting. Scheming. I am of course talking about my fibroids. The little monsters.

If you've got a uterus, and you're listening to this wondering, "What are fibroids?" They're in you. I don't make the rules. These sneaky bald-headed bitches are in 80% of uteruses and most people don't even know. They're growths in the uterus that don't cause cancer and for most people don't even cause problems. But they had it out for me. While most people's fibroids are grape or pea-sized, mine were the size of grapefruits and eggplants. If you're thinking, "Couldn't you feel them? Hasn't that been uncomfortable?" Yes, of course, I could feel them and of course, they were uncomfortable, but I'm a Queer, Black woman with anxiety. I am always uncomfortable. And I told people. I told people constantly. But here's the other thing about being a Queer, Black woman with anxiety: It takes a long time for someone to actually hear you, so you eventually learn to become silent.

The fibroids, however, would not be silenced. They wanted to be seen, perceived, and ungoverned. They grew so large I could no longer ignore them. One day, while masturbating, I discovered these no-necked heifers had grown so large, one of them was blocking my cervix. The fibroids had closed my business without me even knowing. So I turned to my primary care physician … Google.

That was when I found out about fibroids.

I went to a Planned Parenthood and was diagnosed by a very understanding Black woman after specifically asking her to examine me for them. She explained my options with a calm, knowing bedside manner that would've put anyone at ease. Except for me. As soon as she mentioned the various surgeries I would need to remove them, I started bawling. She assured me I wouldn't have to have surgery if I didn't want to. I didn't have to fight them. I could just learn to live with them.

"Take some time to think about what you want to do. There's no need to panic."

I panicked. Suddenly, these hateful, dusty skeezers called "fibroids" became the center of my life. I started doing extensive research. Obviously, by that, I mean doom-scrolling at three in the morning. I started to discover all these things I'd been told to stop complaining about were actually worth complaining about.

My monthly descent into suicidal darkness. Probably not normal. The constant stomach pains, the never-ending peeing, the backaches, the red sea periods that looked like that scene from *The Shining*, all of it was being caused by these lumpy, lopsided, evil-ass fibroids! It was like a bad horror movie.

The call is coming from inside the uterus!

I was ready to fight back! I was ready to take on these fibroids with everything Medicaid had in its arsenal. Then, the pandemic hit, and it was just me and my knock-kneed, no-upper-lip-having ass fibroids. Stuck in the house. No doctors to help me fight them and a whole lot of apocalyptic stress. They got bigger. And, I would say, stronger. By the time COVID restrictions had eased up enough to go to the doctor's again, them bitches were on their hulk-shit.

Doctors tried everything. I had multiple MRIs where I would hear doctors talk about my uterus like she wasn't right there in the room. They called her "gigantic," "warped," "stretched," "extremely large," just reckless. My uterus is from Bed-Stuy, so I know she wanted to take off her ovaries and fight them.

I was given a hormone called Lupron, which gave me menopause symptoms but did nothing to shrink the fibroids. I was just walking around sweating and crying and still filled to the brim with these doofy-looking balls of misshapen pussy meat. I had an extremely painful procedure called a Uterine Artery Embolization that cut the blood supply from the femoral artery to the uterine artery.

This was supposed to starve the fibroids so they died. I woke up during the procedure to one of the radiologists saying, "OH MY GOD, HER UTERUS IS GIGANTIC!" and politely asked to be put back under.

I woke up again to cramps so painful I threw up blood. The pain lasted for weeks, but the fibroids did not die. Those uneven matzo ball-built bitches were stubborn.

The only procedure left was a hysterectomy, a word that scared the shit out of me when it was first recommended, but that I again knew nothing about. I never wanted biological children, but I still thought of a hysterectomy as a failure. An end to a core facet of my womanhood. My dumb ass even asked the doctor if I would grow a mustache after the surgery. After doing a little more research and a lot of mulling over, I accepted that it would be the best option for me. Besides, I've been in the Queer community long enough to know that a uterus does not make a woman.

I found a gynecological surgeon who specialized in laparoscopic hysterectomies on people with large fibroids. I called her "The Big Uterus Whisperer." She was kind and gave me lots of information about what was going to happen and when. When she told me I was keeping my ovaries, I sincerely asked if my eggs would drop out of my coochie without the uterus to keep them inside. She didn't even laugh. She almost did, but she held it in. She was the best surgeon I could've asked for, but I was still pretty sure she would kill me on the table.

I felt frozen with terror about the prospect of having a hysterectomy but shaken at the thought of having to lug around a uterus full of tumors for the rest of my life. I couldn't enjoy life the same.

The fibroids were ever-present in every moment and interaction, but I was the only one who was aware of them. Even joyous occasions were hampered by their presence. When I was passed at my first comedy club, the fibroids were there, knocking on my bladder. When I tried to have penetrative sex, they were guarding the door, not letting nothing in. I had prided myself on my power bottom status and now I couldn't even take strap anymore? These fibroids had blocked my cervix and my blessings. Why was this happening to me? I wanted to fight my fibroids, but those hoes were beating my ass.

I knew if there was anyone to blame, it would be my mother. And in a way, I was right. Fibroids are hereditary. My mom had dealt with them her entire adult life. I had overheard her talking about them with my Aunt Juhnelle and was promptly told to stop minding grown folks' business. But now that grown folks' business was my business, she felt at ease to share a little story.

In her 6th or 7th month of pregnancy, she was told there was a large fibroid blocking her vaginal canal. There would be no way for the fetus to pass through safely and no way to remove it without harming the fetus. They would have to terminate. My mom was heartbroken. But just before the termination date, she felt sudden throbbing, unbearable pain.

She went to the doctor who discovered that her little fetus had grown some big ass feet and kicked the fibroid out of the way. That fetus was me.

Before you ask, yes, that was extremely painful for my mother. My bad. But I was born. Now I pay bills and cry on the subway.

This struggle with fibroids was not new. This was an ancient blood feud. I'd kicked fibroids' asses before I was even born and now, I needed to do it again. I wish I could tell you this story of fetal triumph inspired me to stomp into the operating room ready for battle but that would be bullshit. I was terrified. I walked into the operating room like it was *The Green Mile*. I sobbed right up until they knocked me out for the surgery. It was a six-hour procedure that required two surgical teams. Apparently, one of my fibroids was clutching my appendix so they had to go down together. Some of the surgical tools ripped up my vulva as they were pulling those hard-headed, yuck mouth fibroids out of me. They had to give me so many stitches, my *pussoir* looked like Frankenstein's head. But those ashy, toe knuckle-looking ass fibroids were gone. Victory was mine.

At my follow-up, a month and a half later, I had one thing on my mind: I wanted to see them. I wanted to look those fibroids in the eye and tell them they had lost. My doctor showed me the pictures she'd taken after the surgery. There, on a little blue sheet, were my uterus, my tubes, and those backstabbing fibroids. I stared at them hoping to feel like a victorious conqueror but instead, I just felt a little bit sad.

Have you ever had a mouse in your apartment? The little bastard's been keeping you up, eating your food, and dropping plague turds all over your house for weeks. Then, one day, you catch him. You look at him in the trap, struggling desperately to escape and you just feel sad for him. You realize he's not the enemy you've made him out to be in your mind. Just a sad, fragile creature much like you.

That was how I felt when I saw those fibroids. They weren't these duplicitous monsters trying to destroy me from the inside-out. They were just a reality of my body. They'd been with me for decades, clamoring for attention. Because of them, I had to take my health seriously for the first time in my adult life. I was able to connect with my mother in ways we hadn't been able to since I was a child. They even inspired a pilot and some decent jokes. They weren't the enemy I'd made them out to be. I made my peace, apologized for calling them flubber-built, bootleg Minions, and whispered my final "Goodbye."

This journey isn't over. My pussy is healed but my relationship with my body still needs work. I have to give myself time and space to reconnect with myself after the trauma of two surgeries and a bunch of hormones. I've got a lot of healing to do, but I'm ready for it. So, if you're listening to this and you have fibroids (which you definitely do; I don't make the rules. Go talk to your gynecologist), give those knock-kneed, bloated bitches a big old hug.

Then kill the shit out of them.

VIVA LA CURL-VOLUTION!

MICHELE CARLO

In the 1970s my family survived Vietnam, hippies, Black power, Gay power, Women's Lib, and the infamous 1977 NYC blackout, but sometimes it seemed my family would not survive my favorite aunt, my mom's youngest sister. Her name was Marisol, but I called her *Titi Dulce*, "sweet auntie." And for some in my family, she was *una troublemaker*.

On the outside, she was like most Latinx women of her generation—she married young and had babies—but she also had another calling: To raise the political consciousness of our family. For those of you who didn't live through it, EVERYTHING was political in the 1970s: The number of your POW bracelets, the height of your platform shoes, and the texture of your hair … especially the texture of your hair.

In my large, proud (and sometimes quite loud) Puerto Rican family, you would find light beige, darker beige, brown, and darker brown members whose hair ranged from pin-straight to Afro-texture. And back in the "pre-hippie" early 1960s when I was born, it was not uncommon that, instead of asking if a new baby had two eyes, ten fingers, and ten toes, the burning question would be, "Bad hair or good?"

But all hair was good hair to Titi Dulce—straight, curly, coily, and everything in between—even though her hair manifesto didn't always sit well with my family. One night after coming over she went to say goodnight to my mother, found her in the bathroom wrapping her hair, and said, "Lucy, I can't believe you still wrap your hair in those orange juice cans every night! This isn't 1950 you know; women have choices now. Keeping your curls is an act of protest—you don't need to look 'more American,' we *are* American!" And she tossed her mane of thick, naturally wavy, natural chestnut-brown hair and left.

"Easy for you to say!" said my mom to the closing door. That was the summer I turned 12, when either hormones—or Watergate—turned my acceptably wavy, light auburn childhood hair into a tangled bush of wiry, orange frizz. No comb could go through it without a half-bottle of *Herbal Essence* conditioner. I could have picked it out with an Afro pick, were I allowed one, but that implement was forbidden by my mother, whose only sign her father was half Afro-Latino, was the jet black, tightly coiled, silky hair she wrapped and ironed into submission daily. As for me, my orange bush was gathered every morning into a tight ponytail circled with a perimeter of barrettes and bobby pins in a futile attempt to tame the frizz. No one in my family had hair like mine. When I started school again, I found out no one else did, either.

In those days, public school kids went from grammar school (K through 6th grade), to junior high (7th through 9th), then high school. While the transition from grammar school to 7th grade could be difficult for some kids, it was worse for me because of my hair. I remember Tina and Neecy, Black Pride besties from the projects who treated me as their "pet project." They'd take turns trying to pick out my hair in the locker room before gym class, saying, "Look, it's almost like ours."

And there were Marie and Antoinette, Sicilian-American twins with very curly hair, who at lunchtime would comb out what Tina and Neecy had done and braid me, saying, "Look, it's almost like ours." I accepted their attentions without protest because Tina and Neecy kept razor blades in their Afros, and Marie and Antoinette had penny rolls hid in their scarves (after all, this was The Bronx). Once again, I was almost like everybody and exactly like nobody —just like at home.

One day after school Titi Dulce came to pick us up for a shopping trip and found my mother once again struggling to get my crown of shame subdued enough for public consumption.

"Lucy—let it go! Let Michele's hair go free. We have choices now!"

"Easy for you to say when your daughter has perfect hair like you. *Por favor, nena,* please, sit still!"

That night, my imperfect self prayed to *El Señor,* "God Our Father," to whom I had been taught to turn to in times of trouble: "Dear God, please, please, *please,* let me wake up with normal hair so my mom and the kids at school will leave me alone." The next morning I woke up with my hair still bright orange, still frizzy, and still bushy, and I cried. Because that Monday was the day our class pictures were going to be taken and I didn't want to look like me. Then while sitting in front of the TV with my bowl of Alpha-Bits, watching *Bill Cosby's Fat Albert*, the answer to my prayers appeared during the commercial break like a vision of Christ on a cracker. It was called "Curl Free: The Natural Curl Relaxer for Complete Styling Freedom," and showed beautiful young women with straight, shiny, submissive—and perfect—black, brown, and blonde hair.

"Well, I bet it works on red hair, too," I thought. And I went on a one-child crusade to get my mother to buy and use it on me. To my surprise, she did—and later that day she moved a kitchen chair into our tiny bathroom. She put on her oldest housecoat and a pair of *Playtex Living Dishwashing Gloves* to perform "God's Miracle" on me.

While she mixed it up, I had second, third, and fourth thoughts. For one thing, it stank. Worse than the runover dead dog I once saw in the street, worse than the bathroom after my brother used it, worse than the worst thing you could imagine. It was not just stench, but a sting—even though my mother had opened the bathroom and all the other windows in the apartment wide, our eyes teared and we both started sneezing. My father came in from the kitchen, took one look and sniff, grabbed my brother, and ran out the door. I thought I heard him say, "Good luck."

Did I say the worst thing was the stink? No, it was the sting. The second my mother combed the horrid potion through my hair, my scalp started to itch, ripple, then burn. "Mommy, how long do I have to have this on?" I don't remember what she answered, but about ten minutes in, I started screaming. My mother bent me over the tub and sprayed me from the shower, saying, "DON'T OPEN YOUR EYES OR YOU'LL GO BLIND!"

When I finally dared open them, I almost wished I had gone blind because a stranger stared back at me in the mirror. Yes, my hair was straight all right, and now half the volume, but it smelled like rotting garbage. And I didn't know who I was anymore. That night I prayed to *El Señor* again, saying, "Please, please *puh-leeeeese* give me my real hair back." Only *El Señor* was apparently on holiday because when I woke up, I was still a smelly, straight-haired stranger, and I cried again.

No matter how many times we washed my hair that weekend or how much *Shalimar* perfume my mom sprayed over me, the malodor still lingered. When Monday came, I had to go back to school and take my picture.

But before the pictures was gym class, where Tina and Neecy looked at me in shock. "What did you do?! You look white now!"

"My mom made me," I said. I mean what could I say? That I brought this travesty upon myself? When it was time for the photos, the photographer held a tissue over his nose as I stared straight ahead and tried not to cry again. But worse came at lunchtime when Marie and Antoinette squealed, "Oh, how pretty!" They whipped out their combs without even noticing the smell. But after a minute Marie screamed, dropped her comb, and ran away. I looked down and saw it on the ground with a big clump of hair in it and looked back up to see Antoinette holding the other comb with an even bigger clump. "Go home, quick, before you die!" she croaked before she, too, ran off.

I ran home as fast as I could because I did not want to die in the street like that poor dead dog. After my mother had rewashed, conditioned, and combed through my hair again, I looked in the mirror and thought I would die. My once shoulder-length hair was now patchy and asymmetrical—ten years before I would wear a similar style as a defiant art student.

"We have to cut it off, *nena*. It's the only way." So out came the good scissors and by the time my mother was done, I had what people called a "pixie," or close enough. I went back to school. The stink finally faded and within two weeks new hair started to grow back in, still wiry, still curly, still orange, but never again at that volume level—and no one played "beauty parlor" on me ever again. It was a miracle.

Another miracle happened. My mother finally stopped fighting with her hair … somewhat … and started using a new *ConAir* blow dryer to create soft waves where once tight coils had been. When Titi Dulce next came over and saw my mother, she nodded her approval. When she saw me, she didn't even blink. She just hugged me and said, "All revolutions have to end sometime. Choices have to be made. Sometimes it's not easy. But I'm glad to see you're finally making your own."

My mother is now in her 80s and wears her soft white hair natural. Titi Dulce is in her 70s. She recently chose to stop dyeing her "natural chestnut" hair and can't wait until it grows back "real." As for me, my hair is still just like me: Almost like everybody, exactly like nobody … and it submits to no one.

CONTRIBUTORS

Nancy Agabian is the author of *The Fear of Large and Small Nations*, a finalist for the 2016 PEN/Bellwether Prize for Socially-Engaged Fiction and forthcoming from Nauset Press in December 2022. Her other books include *Me as her again: True Stories of an Armenian Daughter,* a memoir, and *Princess Freak*, a collection of poetry and performance art texts. In 2021 she was awarded Lambda Literary Foundation's Jeanne Cordova Prize for Lesbian/Queer Nonfiction. A longtime teacher of creative writing, she is currently leading classes at Grub Street.

Nancy's mother, Sylvia Agabian, passed away suddenly in August 2022 as this anthology was nearing completion.

"This essay is published in honor of my mother and her love of the arts. Writing about faith gave me an opportunity to process some of the ambiguous grief of losing my mother to dementia. I am grateful to *NYTI* for accompanying me on multiple steps of my care-giving journey."

Fred Backus was born and raised in Westchester County, NY and has been an actor and musician in New York City for the past thirty years. In the early 1990s, he was the guitarist for New York City punk band the Casualties, He now lives in Astoria, New York with his wife and daughter.**Colby Black** is your typical certified private investigator in South Dakota, who's based in Brooklyn, New York. He's also a registered wedding officiant. So it's Rev. Colby Black, P.I., to you, pal. He's also been producing advertising for 22 years while plotting his escape from the industry.

Michele Carlo is a writer, storyteller (and sometime actor) who has told stories across the U.S., including the MOTH's *Mainstage in NYC*, the *RISK!* and *Story Collider* live shows and podcasts, on NPR and the

WGBH-PBS series "Stories from the Stage." She is also the author of the NYC-set memoir *Fish Out Of Agua* and is a contributor to several literary anthologies. michelecarlo.com

Letisia Cruz is a Cuban-American writer and artist. She is the author of *The Lost Girls Book of Divination* (Tolsun Books, 2018). Her writing and artwork have appeared in *[PANK], Ninth Letter, The Acentos Review, Gulf Stream, Saw Palm, Third Coast, Duende, Moko Caribbean Arts & Letters, 300 Days of Sun, Black Fox Literary Magazine, Ink Brick,* and *Sakura Review,* among others. She is a graduate of Fairleigh Dickinson University's MFA program and currently lives in St. Petersburg, Florida with her partner and their cats, plants and several hundred lizards.

Noah Diamond has participated in *No, YOU Tell It!* as a storyteller, and has assisted with virtual *NYTI* events. His theatre work includes *I'll Say She Is,* the lost Marx Brothers musical, which he restored and adapted, and played the role of Groucho in the show's first-ever revival, at the New York International Fringe Festival in 2014 and Off Broadway at the Connelly Theater in 2016. He has appeared as Groucho Marx in dozens of other projects, and produced a trilogy of documentaries for SUNY Fredonia's annual Marx Brothers festival. He can be heard monthly as a co-host of *The Marx Brothers Council Podcast, Beyond the Marxes.* Noah wrote, designed, produced, and/or performed in *Quarantigone* (2020 virtual production), *400 Years in Manhattan* (United Solo Theatre Festival, 2019), and the Nero Fiddled political musicals. His books include *Love Marches On, 400 Years in Manhattan,* and *Gimme a Thrill.* noahdiamond.com

Mike Dressel is a writer based in New York. His work has appeared in *Nude Bruce Review, Warm Brothers, Bachelors, Newfound, Your Impossible Voice, Chelsea Station,* and *Vol. 1 Brooklyn,* among others, as well as in the anthologies *Best Gay Stories 2016* and *Best Gay Stories 2017.* For eight years he was a creative team member of *No, YOU Tell It!* He has been a National Endowment for the Humanities Summer Scholar and the recipient of writing fellowships from The Sundress Academy for the Arts and The Edward F. Albee Foundation.

Ellie Dvorkin Dunn is an entertainer/writer/host who has been hailed as "outrageous" by *The New York Times* and "ready for prime time" by *The New York Post*. Her storytelling has been featured in shows such as *Risk!, Generation Women,* and *No, YOU Tell It!,* and her writing has been published in *Dame Magazine* and the soon-to-be-released book *Moms Who Kill*, a collection of essays by comedians who also happen to be mothers. Her most recent project is co-producing *Circling the Drain, a Perimenopausal Podcast About the Period Before You Stop Getting Your Period.* Please listen and subscribe!

H.E. Fisher is the author of the collection Sterile Field (Free Lines Press, 2022). Her chapbook, JANE ALMOST ALWAYS SMILES is forthcoming from Moonstone Press in September 2022.
H.E.'s poems, prose poems, and essays have appeared in *The Rumpus, Whale Road Review, Indianapolis Review, The Hopper, Miracle Monocle, Anti-Heroin Chic, Miracle Monocle, Longleaf Review, Barren Magazine,* and *Canary,* among other publications. H.E. was awarded the 2019 Stark Poetry Prize in Memory of Raymond Patterson at City College of New York, was a finalist in the 2020-21 Comstock Review Chapbook Contest, and has been nominated for Best of the Net. H.E. is the editor of *(Re) An Ideas Journal*. Her work can be found at: hefisher.com.

Kelly Jean Fitzsimmons is a writer, educator, and storyteller who lives in Astoria, Queens. Her nonfiction work has appeared in *HiLoBrow, Human Parts, Marie Claire,* and *Hippocampus Magazine,* among others. Her most recent play, a superhero comedy, *All I Want Is One More Meanwhile...* made its Midwest premiere at Otherworld Theatre in Chicago. After a decade of supporting AP teachers and coordinators behind the scenes with the Advanced Placement Program at the College Board, she stepped back into the classroom. Now she designs and teaches writing workshops for students of all ages. Her specialty is helping high school students craft meaningful college application essays that highlight their unique character for admissions officers. Earning an MFA in Creative Nonfiction from Fairleigh Dickinson University, Kelly Jean combined her love for theater and narrative nonfiction to create *No, YOU Tell It!* Subscribe to the podcast at noyoutellit.com, or your preferred platform, and share it with a friend!

E. James Ford is a performer, writer, and designer based in NYC. On TV, he has appeared on *Gotham* as an Arkham Asylum inmate who was co-murdered by The Penguin and The Joker, on *Happy!* as a psychotic easter bunny, and on *Pioneer One* as a hapless Homeland Security agent. Favorite NYC theater roles include *The Dreary Coast* (dir. by Jeff Stark, NY Times Theatre Pick), *Biter: Everytime I Turn Around* (title:point, Time Out NY Best of the Year), *Private Manning Goes to Washington* (The Representatives), and *The Girl Who Handcuffed Houdini* (dir. by Cynthia von Buhler). As a voiceover actor he can be heard on the animated *Pokémon*, *Toy Cop*, *The Donkey King*, and *The Christmas Witch*.

Alexandra Gray (she/her) is a writer and performer whose work has been staged at Dixon Place, St. Ann's Warehouse, La MaMa, One Arm Red, HERE Arts Center, and IRT Theater, among other beloved indie venues. Her performing roots are in devised physical theater; with Six Characters, Synaesthetic Theatre, and Booby Hatch, she co-created numerous evening-length shows, three award-winning video shorts, and a 30-minute TV pilot. Alex's writing has been featured in the *Huffington Post*, *Girl Crush Zine* (editors Jenna Wortham and Thessaly La Force), the regretfully-defunct Gorgeous Ladies of Comedy website (theGLOC.net), and *No, YOU Tell It!* She is pursuing an MFA in Playwriting at Augsburg University.

Nicole Greevy is an award-winning poet, playwright and podcaster. Born and raised in South Central Pennsylvania, she now lives in New York City where, as writer and producer (and the voice of Sheriff Jane Rowland) for the hit horror-comedy anthology podcast *Uncanny County*, she gets ample opportunity to put her childhood pop-culture nerdiness to use. She lives with her husband and son, who, although he has outgrown it, still has his felt Wonder Woman tiara. She is grateful to *No, YOU Tell It!* for inspiring some of the best writing experiences of her life.

Rebecca Hart is a NYC-based actor, musician, and writer. She is the librettist/lyricist for *IRON JOHN: an american ghost story* (NAMT Festival 2019; Richard Rodgers Award Finalist) and the short-form opera *the barren(s)* (Kennedy Center /American Opera Initiative commission). Her songs have appeared in productions at BAM, The Public, the National Theatre of Oslo, Gloucester Stage, Woolly Mammoth, and the Village Theatre; her album *The Magician's Daughter* is available on all streaming services. She currently writes the weekly substack newsletter *from the chrysalis* and recently released the memoir/manifesto *Respect For Tarot: a new way of seeing* as a free download. Performance dates and further info at rebeccahart.net

Brian Hutchinson is a part-time martial arts performer and voice actor who has been living in New York City for 15 years. After a long hiatus he is actually considering buying another car on eBay. He can be reached for comment, advice or discouragement at triplebzus@gmail.com.

Erika Iverson is a New York based theatre artist, writer and storyteller. She is proud to be part of the creative team at *No, YOU Tell It!* where she serves as director, dramaturg, and cheerleader for non-linear storytelling. Thanks to her association with La MaMa ETC, Erika was able to act in Germany, to create an original dance theatre piece in Italy, and to perform Ionesco's *The Lesson* in the country of the playwright's birth, Romania. Erika has also performed at The Cornelia Street Café, the Abington Theatre Company, The Knitting Factory, and Judson Street Church. She has created original roles as a featured actor with the Magis Theatre Company and This Is Not A Theatre Company. In addition to her work with *No, YOU Tell It!* she has directed shows for One Woman Standing and the United Solo Festival. She is deeply grateful to Kelly Jean Fitzsimmons for creating *No, YOU Tell It!* and for giving her an artistic home for all these years. Long live *No, YOU Tell It!*

Heather Lang-Cassera is a 2022 Nevada Arts Council Fellow and was the 2019-2021 Clark County, Nevada, Poet Laureate. Heather serves Nevada State College as a Lecturer teaching College Success and Creative Writing and as a Faculty Advisor for their literary magazine, *300 Days of Sun*. She is a Publisher and Editor for Tolsun Books. Her poems and stories have been published in *Las Vegas Writes, Lumina, The Normal School, North American Review, Paper Darts, South Dakota Review,* and elsewhere. Her full-length collection of poems, *Gathering Broken Light,* was published in 2021 with Unsolicited Press. heatherlang.cassera.net

Tim Lindner is a copywriter, poet, and college Writing Instructor at Middlesex College. He's published poems in *300 Days of Sun, The Citron Review, The Northern Virginia Review* and more. He also owns a small business, Revisionary Writing and Editing LLC, where he helps people write their resumes, college essays, books and more. He's been helping *No, YOU Tell It!* since 2020 as a co-producer, social media content creator, and storytelling coach for the program's virtual and in-person shows. Along with this anthology, he's editing a collection of stories and poems about death and grieving to be published by Tolsun Books in 2023.

Charlotte Marchant is a writer who has a blog using response to letters written by her father to her during the tumultuous sixties and a radio performance dialoguing with the letters and several storytelling events. She's currently working on turning her blog into a memoir. At the age of 73, she admits to confronting the reality of her mortality as there are less years ahead. She considers herself a radical despite not having yet figured out how to manifest it concretely as an elder. She deeply cares about the world and feels the weight of that concern on a daily basis.

Sheria Mattis is a Queer, Brooklyn-born comedian, writer, actress, and awkward Black girl. She has written for *Reductress, Cash App, Netflix is a Joke*, Leslie Jones, Fran Drescher, and Abby Terkuhle.

Heather Quinlan is a writer and filmmaker whose feature-length documentary on the New York accent, *If These Knishes Could Talk*, was covered in The New Yorker, The New York Times, WSJ, and the BBC and screened at the Library of Congress. In addition, Quinlan recently wrote *Plagues, Pandemics, and Viruses: From the Plague of Athens to COVID-19*, published by Visible Ink Press. She is now producing and directing *Staten Island Graveyard*, about an African-American cemetery that was paved over and turned into a parking lot. Quinlan lives in New Jersey with her husband, writer Adam McGovern.

Tazio Ruffilo is a born and bred product of Paterson, New Jersey, where he was raised by his jack-of-all-arts dad, undefeatable mom, and desperado big sister. The different hats he's worn and the cast of characters in his hometown are major influences on his writing. Tazio holds an MA in History and MFA in Creative Writing from Fairleigh Dickinson University. He teaches writing and communications at Hudson County Community College.

Amanda Sisk has participated in *No, YOU Tell It!* as a storyteller and director. Recent credits include directing and performing in the virtual play *Quarantigone*; and producing and directing *400 Years in Manhattan* (Best Educational Show, 2019 United Solo Theatre Festival). In 2016, she directed the Off Broadway production of *I'll Say She Is* (New York Times Critic's Pick). Other New York credits include co-writing and directing the Nero Fiddled political musicals (2004-2008), and appearing in *Orestes 2.0* (HERE Arts Center), *Tecmessa* (The Kitchen), and *Superhero* at the 2009 Chester Horn Short Play Festival (Best Actress Award). She is the recipient of one Backstage Bistro Award and three Memphis Theatre Awards. Most days, she can be found banging her head against desks in advertising agencies.

Marcos Stafne (he/him) is a proud alumni of *No, YOU Tell It!* His first *NYTI* story, "The Anxiety of Emptiness," was featured in the *Urban Dwellers* show, "Snake Dreams" was written for the first alumni performance, and most recently, "Imaginary Rules" was part of *Defiant*, the first live show of 2021. Marcos has been working for various museums, zoos, and aquariums for the past 25 years or so, and writes extensively for museum blogs and scholarly journals.

Sokunthary Svay is a Khmer writer from the Bronx. A founding member of the Cambodian American Literary Arts Association (CALAA), she has received fellowships from the American Opera Project, Poets House, Willow Books, and CUNY. In addition to a published poetry collection, *Apsara in New York* (Willow Books, 2017), her first opera, *Woman of Letters*, set by composer Liliya Ugay, received its world premiere at the Kennedy Center in January 2020. Her second opera with Ugay, *Chhlong Tonle*, received its premiere in March 2022. She is a doctoral candidate in English at the CUNY Graduate Center.

Molly Touger is a Bostonian turned Brooklynite who has, over the course of her career, worked as a journalist, barista, publicist, kayak guide and instructional designer. She is currently pursuing an MFA in creative writing through SUNY Stony Brook.

Sha-Née Williams (pronounced *Sha-Nay*) is a Brooklyn-based artist, gamer, and lover of all things comics. Her work revolves around telling stories through serious, whimsical, fantastical, and sci-fi imagery. With watercolors as her main medium, she loves working traditionally. She enjoys sketching and illustrating ideas that come to mind. She grew up playing games that had fantastical worlds such as the *Final Fantasy Series*, *Tomb Raider*, and *Xenosaga Series*. She also enjoys reading comics and watching shows such as *Justice League* and the *Star Trek Series*. Being exposed to this genre of media as a child and well into adulthood, influenced her as an artist to create. Her goal is to tell her stories and share them with others. shaneewilliamsart.squarespace.com

Jeff Wills is a forty-something father of two working in arts administration, but also a former actor, clown, and circus performer. He has been a featured reader for *Liars' League NYC* and *The Literary Review* (*TLR*). While most of Jeff's professional writing has taken the form of scripts for original theatrical productions, he has written narrative fiction for almost his entire life. In 2018 he achieved a life goal in writing a 120,000-word fantasy novel. *The Spinning Wheel* tells the story of fairy tales as they actually happened—and the further tales of those fairies responsible.

Kent D. Wolf is a founding partner and agent at Neon Literary. Originally from rural Illinois, he lives in Manhattan with his husband and two cats.

THE MOST BEAUTIFUL INSANITY

South Beach Crime Thriller Series, Book One
Heather Wilde

"(Wilde's) unusual lyricism stamps her characters and their sordid choices with authenticity. The result is an insider's lens on the grislier truths behind beauty and privilege." —**The Miami Herald**

The fashion world is turned upside-down with the overdose death of a young wannabe. Police scrutiny exposes the debauchery of today's modeling biz...

To Learn More, Visit Amazon Today.

SWEET DEMON LOVE BABY

South Beach Crime Thriller Series, Book Two
Heather Wilde

"It's rare, exceedingly rare to find a relatively new author with such honed skills. The scenes and characters came to life for me as I found myself drawn hopelessly into the story." —Phillip P Macko, author of The Conduit

Trace Strickland is a male dancer turned homicide detective. When his stripper girlfriend is found murdered in South Beach, he becomes the prime suspect.

To Learn More, Visit Amazon Today.

WHAT HAPPENED AT SISTERS CREEK

A Horror Novel
Lee Anderson

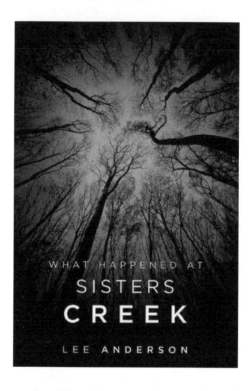

A small town sherrif sends a search party into the woods to hunt two escape convicts. What they find instead is a savage, unthinkable horror...

"I squirmed, I cringed, I gritted my teeth and held my breath...And that ending.... I just.... WHAT? I don't even know what to say. Amazing? Exhilarating? Nerve-racking? Total WTF moment? It was soooooo good!" —Jessica Scurlock, author of **Pretty Lies**

To Learn More, Visit Amazon Today.

BACHELOR'S GUIDE TO POST-APOCALYPTIC SUCCESS

Book One of the Post-Apocalyptic Bachelor Guides
Rory Penland

Finding love after the world has ended is hard...

Brandon Hoffner is a forty-something ex-baseball star and entrepreneur. He awakens from cryo-sleep to discover the world has suffered a nuclear holocaust, seemingly wiping out all human life on Earth. With his new dog Beau, Hoffner sails the world, seeking other possible survivors, hoping at best to find someone he can continue the human race with.

To Learn More, Visit Amazon Today.

Made in the USA
Middletown, DE
22 September 2022

10992676R00168